At Issue

| Pipelines and Politics

Other Books in the At Issue Series

At Issue

| Pipelines and Politics

Lisa Idzikowski, Book Editor

GREENHAVEN
PUBLISHING

Published in 2018 by Greenhaven Publishing, LLC
353 3rd Avenue, Suite 255, New York, NY 10010

Copyright © 2018 by Greenhaven Publishing, LLC

First Edition

Cover image: sumkinn/Shutterstock.com

Library of Congress Cataloging-in-Publication Data

Names: Idzikowski, Lisa, editor.
Title: Pipelines and politics / Lisa Idzikowski, book editor.
Description: First edition. | New York : Greenhaven Publishing, [2018] |
  Series: At issue | Includes bibliographical references and index. | Audience: Grades 9-
  12.
Identifiers: LCCN 2017036649| ISBN 9781534502031 (library bound) | ISBN
  9781534502123 (pbk.)
Subjects: LCSH: Petroleum pipelines--Political aspects--United
  States--Juvenile literature. | Natural gas pipeline--Political
  aspects--United States--Juvenile literature. | Petroleum industry and
  trade--Political aspects--United States--Juvenile literature. | Gas
  industry--Political aspects--United States--Juvenile literature.
Classification: LCC HD9580.U5 P56 2018 | DDC 388.50973--dc23
LC record available at https://lccn.loc.gov/2017036649

Manufactured in the United States of America

Website: http://greenhavenpublishing.com

Contents

Introduction

The worldwide daily consumption and usage of various types of energy is undeniably increasing. Individuals, families, businesses, communities and countries use varying degrees of energy, with developed nations typically using larger amounts than non-developed areas. How informed are consumers when it comes to the production and distribution of energy and energy products?

One assumption is that people generally want, need, and even expect the benefits of energy produced by fossil fuels and the products made from these materials. What many people find objectionable is the positioning of pipelines used to transport fossil fuels—for assorted reasons they don't want them located in or nearby their communities and backyards. From the Keystone XL pipeline—according to a 2017 Pew Research Center survey, only four-in-ten people support its construction—to the British Petroleum offshore oil well disaster and frequent ocean tanker spills, it is the transportation of oil and natural gas that create the most controversy.

Humans have been using fossil fuels to their benefit since Stone Age hunter-gatherers used a type of sticky surface tar or pitch to construct arrowhead tipped arrows, and the Egyptians mummified individuals with a chemical mixture that included bitumen, a form of oil. Fossil fuels—including coal, crude oil, and natural gas—were formed 280 to 345 million years ago during the Carboniferous geologic period. Dead and decaying plant and animal remains sandwiched between layers of mud, sand, and silt, weighted down, and under extreme pressure in the earth's crust for hundreds of millions of years produced this non-renewable hydrocarbon resource.

Today, fossil fuel industries drill or mine for these finite energy sources, burn them to produce electricity, or refine them into petroleum. Together, these commodities power the world's automobiles, airplanes, and an array of transportation vehicles. Fuel is also used to heat homes, and an ingredient for a multitude of items such as plastics, solvents, medicines, and personal care products—including shampoo, toothpaste, and bandages. Even computers and crayons depend on petroleum for their manufacture.

Such increased consumption of energy means transportation of both oil and natural gas must increase along with its production. Both Canada and the United States realize this and consequently are moving to design and construct additional pipelines. A study by Canada's Fraser Institute demonstrates that pipelines are "without a doubt the safest way to transport oil and gas," and the Canadian Energy Pipeline Association reports that Canadian companies transport "1.2 billion barrels of oil and almost 5.4 trillion cubic feet of natural gas per year with a 99.999 per cent safety record," and that Canada's mainline transmission system had no safety incidents in 2015.

Proponents of pipelines, and of increased production and transportation of fossil fuels in the United States, cite various advantages accounting for their endorsements. Supporters point to the fact that finding ways to decrease America's dependence on Middle Eastern oil would positively affect security concerns, and energy availability. Those in favor also cite the probable lower prices for consumers, which in turn provide economic advantages for the country.

According to the American Petroleum Institute, the largest network of energy pipelines is located in the U.S. "America depends on a network of more than 207,800 miles of liquids pipelines, over 300,000 miles of gas transmission pipelines, and more than 2.1 million miles of gas distribution pipelines to safely and efficiently move energy and raw materials to fuel our nation's economic engine," says the API. And U.S. President Donald Trump insists that a benefit of pipelines will be a "lot of jobs, 28,000 jobs," including "great construction jobs."

However, opponents of an enhanced pipeline network and construction agenda outline numerous environmental concerns—

especially contamination of water supplies and decreasing air quality. They insist that animals and their habitats would be put in danger—endangered whooping cranes would be at risk "of flying into new power lines that would be constructed to keep oil pumping through the Keystone XL" according to the National Wildlife Federation. Pipeline protestors maintain that investment in the fossil fuel industry will stifle research and development of alternative energy sources such as wind, solar, biomass and other new technologies. In certain locations, pipeline development directly impinges on Native American lands and tribes are putting up a valiant fight to save sacred burial sites, their land and water, and treaty rights as sovereign nations.

Energy consumption, production and transportation is a complex issue with serious global implications. It is matter of concern with committed proponents and vocal opponents, as the following viewpoints in *At Issue: Pipelines and Politics* illustrate.

1

A Complex Network of Pipelines Successfully Transports Natural Gas

NaturalGas.org

NaturalGas.org is an educational website designed to educate students, teachers, industry members, government personnel, and the media about the many aspects of the natural gas industry.

In the following informative write-up from a valued natural gas resource site, we learn about the extensive network of pipelines that connects natural gas producers to consumers. The pipeline transportation network is concerned with the various components of pipeline construction, the technology to monitor the system, and the protocol used to maintain safety.

The efficient and effective movement of natural gas from producing regions to consumption regions requires an extensive and elaborate transportation system. In many instances, natural gas produced from a particular well will have to travel a great distance to reach its point of use. The transportation system for natural gas consists of a complex network of pipelines, designed to quickly and efficiently transport natural gas from its origin, to areas of high natural gas demand. Transportation of natural gas is closely linked to its storage: should the natural gas being transported not be immediately required, it can be put into storage facilities for when it is needed.

"The Transportation of Natural Gas," by NaturalGas.org, September 20, 2013. Reprinted by Permission.

There are three major types of pipelines along the transportation route: the gathering system, the interstate pipeline system, and the distribution system. The gathering system consists of low pressure, small diameter pipelines that transport raw natural gas from the wellhead to the processing plant. Should natural gas from a particular well have high sulfur and carbon dioxide contents (sour gas), a specialized sour gas gathering pipe must be installed. Sour gas is corrosive, thus its transportation from the wellhead to the sweetening plant must be done carefully.

Pipelines can be characterized as interstate or intrastate. Interstate pipelines are similar to in the interstate highway system: they carry natural gas across state boundaries, in some cases clear across the country. Intrastate pipelines, on the other hand, transport natural gas within a particular state. This section will cover only the fundamentals of interstate natural gas pipelines, however the technical and operational details discussed are essentially the same for intrastate pipelines.

Interstate Natural Gas Pipelines

The interstate natural gas pipeline network transports processed natural gas from processing plants in producing regions to those areas with high natural gas requirements, particularly large, populated urban areas. As can be seen, the pipeline network extends across the entire country.

Interstate pipelines are the "highways" of natural gas transmission. Natural gas that is transported through interstate pipelines travels at high pressure in the pipeline, at pressures anywhere from 200 to 1500 pounds per square inch (psi). This reduces the volume of the natural gas being transported (by up to 600 times), as well as propelling natural gas through the pipeline.

This section will cover the components of the interstate pipeline system, the construction of pipelines, and pipeline inspection and safety.

Pipeline Components

Interstate pipelines consist of a number of components that ensure the efficiency and reliability of a system that delivers such an important energy source year-round, twenty-four hours a day, and includes a number of different components.

Transmission Pipes

Transmission pipes can measure anywhere from 6 to 48 inches in diameter, depending on their function. Certain component pipe sections can even consist of small diameter pipe, as small as 0.5 inches in diameter. However, this small diameter pipe is usually used only in gathering and distribution systems. Mainline transmission pipes, the principle pipeline in a given system, are usually between 16 and 48 inches in diameter. Lateral pipelines, which deliver natural gas to or from the mainline, are typically between 6 and 16 inches in diameter. Most major interstate pipelines are between 24 and 36 inches in diameter. The actual pipeline itself, commonly called "line pipe," consists of a strong carbon steel material, engineered to meet standards set by the American Petroleum Institute (API). In contrast, some distribution pipe is made of highly advanced plastic, because of the need for flexibility, versatility and the ease of replacement.

Transmission pipelines are produced in steel mills, which are sometimes specialized to produce only pipeline. There are two different production techniques, one for small diameter pipes and one for large diameter pipes. For large diameter pipes, from 20 to 42 inches in diameter, the pipes are produced from sheets of metal which are folded into a tube shape, with the ends welded together to form a pipe section. Small diameter pipe, on the other hand, can be produced seamlessly. This involves heating a metal bar to very high temperatures, then punching a hole through the middle of the bar to produce a hollow tube. In either case, the pipe is tested before being shipped from the steel mill, to ensure that it can meet the pressure and strength standards for transporting natural gas.

Line pipe is also covered with a specialized coating to ensure that it does not corrode once placed in the ground. The purpose of the coating is to protect the pipe from moisture, which causes corrosion and rusting. There are a number of different coating techniques. In the past, pipelines were coated with specialized coal tar enamel. Today, pipes are often protected with what is known as a fusion bond epoxy, which gives the pipe a noticeable light blue color. In addition, cathodic protection is often used; which is a technique of running an electric current through the pipe to ward off corrosion and rusting.

Compressor Stations

As mentioned, natural gas is highly pressurized as it travels through an interstate pipeline. To ensure that the natural gas flowing through any one pipeline remains pressurized, compression of this natural gas is required periodically along the pipe. This is accomplished by compressor stations, usually placed at 40 to 100 mile intervals along the pipeline. The natural gas enters the compressor station, where it is compressed by either a turbine, motor, or engine.

Turbine compressors gain their energy by using up a small proportion of the natural gas that they compress. The turbine itself serves to operate a centrifugal compressor, which contains a type of fan that compresses and pumps the natural gas through the pipeline. Some compressor stations are operated by using an electric motor to turn the same type of centrifugal compressor. This type of compression does not require the use of any of the natural gas from the pipe, however it does require a reliable source of electricity nearby. Reciprocating natural gas engines are also used to power some compressor stations. These engines resemble a very large automobile engine, and are powered by natural gas from the pipeline. The combustion of the natural gas powers pistons on the outside of the engine, which serves to compress the natural gas.

In addition to compressing natural gas, compressor stations also usually contain some type of liquid separator, much like the ones used to dehydrate natural gas during its processing. Usually, these separators consist of scrubbers and filters that capture any liquids or other unwanted particles from the natural gas in the pipeline. Although natural gas in pipelines is considered "dry" gas, it is not uncommon for a certain amount of water and hydrocarbons to condense out of the gas stream while in transit. The liquid separators at compressor stations ensure that the natural gas in the pipeline is as pure as possible, and usually filter the gas prior to compression.

Metering Stations

In addition to compressing natural gas to reduce its volume and push it through the pipe, metering stations are placed periodically along interstate natural gas pipelines. These stations allow pipeline companies to monitor the natural gas in their pipes. Essentially, these metering stations measure the flow of gas along the pipeline, and allow pipeline companies to "track" natural gas as it flows along the pipeline. These metering stations employ specialized meters to measure the natural gas as it flows through the pipeline, without impeding its movement.

Valves

Interstate pipelines include a great number of valves along their entire length. These valves work like gateways; they are usually open and allow natural gas to flow freely, or they can be used to stop gas flow along a certain section of pipe. There are many reasons why a pipeline may need to restrict gas flow in certain areas. For example, if a section of pipe requires replacement or maintenance, valves on either end of that section of pipe can be closed to allow engineers and work crews safe access. These large valves can be placed every 5 to 20 miles along the pipeline, and are subject to regulation by safety codes.

Control Stations and SCADA Systems

Natural gas pipeline companies have customers on both ends of the pipeline—the producers and processors that input gas into the pipeline, and the consumers and local gas utilities that take gas out of the pipeline. In order to manage the natural gas that enters the pipeline, and to ensure that all customers receive timely delivery of their portion of this gas, sophisticated control systems are required to monitor the gas as it travels through all sections of what could be a very lengthy pipeline network. To accomplish this task of monitoring and controlling the natural gas that is traveling through the pipeline, centralized gas control stations collect, assimilate, and manage data received from monitoring and compressor stations all along the pipe.

Most of the data that is received by a control station is provided by Supervisory Control and Data Acquisition (SCADA) systems. These systems are essentially sophisticated communications systems that take measurements and collect data along the pipeline (usually in a metering or compressor stations and valves) and transmit it to the centralized control station. Flow rate through the pipeline, operational status, pressure, and temperature readings may all be used to assess the status of the pipeline at any one time. These systems also work in real time, meaning that there is little lag time between the measurements taken along the pipeline and their transmission to the control station.

The data is relayed to a centralized control station, allowing pipeline engineers to know exactly what is happening along the pipeline at all times. This enables quick reactions to equipment malfunctions, leaks, or any other unusual activity along the pipeline. Some SCADA systems also incorporate the ability to remotely operate certain equipment along the pipeline, including compressor stations, allowing engineers in a centralized control center to immediately and easily adjust flow rates in the pipeline.

Pipeline Construction

As natural gas use increases, so does the need to have transportation infrastructure in place to supply the increased demand. This means that pipeline companies are constantly assessing the flow of natural gas across the U.S., and building pipelines to allow transportation of natural gas to those areas that are underserved.

Constructing natural gas pipelines requires a great deal of planning and preparation. In addition to actually building the pipeline, several permitting and regulatory processes must be completed. In many cases, prior to beginning the permitting and land access processes, natural gas pipeline companies prepare a feasibility analysis to ensure that an acceptable route for the pipeline exists that provides the least impact to the environment and public infrastructure already in place.

Assuming a pipeline company obtains all the required permits and satisfies all of the regulatory requirements, construction of the pipe may begin. Extensive surveying of the intended route is completed, both aerial and land based, to ensure that no surprises pop up during actual assembly of the pipeline.

Installing a pipeline is much like an assembly line process, with sections of the pipeline being completed in stages. First, the path of the pipeline is cleared of all removable impediments, including trees, boulders, brush, and anything else that may prohibit the construction. Once the pipeline's path has been cleared sufficiently to allow construction equipment to gain access, sections of pipes are laid out along the intended path, a process called "stringing" the pipe. These pipe sections are commonly from 40 to 80 feet long, and are specific to their destination. That is, certain areas have different requirements for coating material and pipe thickness.

Once the pipe is in place, trenches are dug alongside the laid out pipe. These trenches are typically five to six feet deep, as the regulations require the pipe to be at least 30 inches below the surface. In certain areas, however, including road crossings and bodies of water, the pipe is buried even deeper. Once the trenches are dug, the pipe is assembled and contoured. This includes welding the sections of pipe together into one continuous pipeline, and bending it slightly, if needed, to fit the contour of the pipeline's path.

Coating is applied to the ends of the pipes. The coating applied at a coating mill typically leaves the ends of the pipe clean, so as not to interfere with welding. Finally, the entire coating of the pipe is inspected to ensure that it is free from defects.

Once the pipe is welded, bent, coated, and inspected it can be lowered into the previously-dug trenches. This is done with specialized construction equipment acting to lift the pipe in a level manner and lower it into the trench. Once lowered into the ground, the trench is filled in carefully, to ensure that the pipe and its coating retain their integrity. The last step in pipeline construction is the hydrostatic test. This consists of running water, at pressures higher than will be needed for natural gas transportation, through the entire length of the pipe. This serves as a test to ensure that the pipeline is strong enough, and absent of any leaks or fissures, before natural gas is pumped through the pipeline.

Laying pipe across streams or rivers can be accomplished in one of two ways. Open cut crossing involves the digging of trenches on the floor of the river to house the pipe. When this is done, the pipe itself is usually fitted with a concrete casing, which both ensures that the pipe stays on the bottom of the river and adds an extra protective coating to prevent any natural gas leaks into the water. Alternatively, a form of directional drilling may be employed, in which a "tunnel" is drilled under the river through which the pipe may be passed. The same techniques are used for road crossings—either an open trench is excavated across the road and replaced once the pipe is installed, or a tunnel may be drilled underneath the road.

Once the pipeline has been installed and covered, extensive efforts are taken to restore the pipeline's pathway to its original state, or to mitigate any environmental or other impacts that may have occurred during the construction process. These steps often include replacing topsoil, fences, irrigation canals, and anything else that may have been removed or upset during the construction process.

Pipeline Inspection and Safety

In order to ensure the efficient and safe operation of the extensive network of natural gas pipelines, pipeline companies routinely inspect their pipelines for corrosion and defects. This is done through the use of sophisticated pieces of equipment known as "smart pigs." Smart pigs are intelligent robotic devices that are propelled down pipelines to evaluate the interior of the pipe. Smart pigs can test pipe thickness, and roundness, check for signs of corrosion, detect minute leaks, and any other defect along the interior of the pipeline that may either impede the flow of gas, or pose a potential safety risk to the operation of the pipeline. Sending a smart pig down a pipeline is fittingly known as "pigging" the pipeline.

In addition to inspection with smart pigs, there are a number of safety precautions and procedures in place to minimize the risk of accidents. In fact, the transportation of natural gas is one of the safest ways of transporting energy, mostly due to the fact that the infrastructure is fixed, and buried underground. According to the Department of Transportation (DOT), pipelines are the safest method of transporting petroleum and natural gas. While there are in excess of 100 deaths per year associated with electric transmission lines, according to the DOT's Office of Pipeline Safety in 2009, there were 0 deaths associated with transmission pipelines, and 10 deaths associated with distribution systems. To learn more about pipeline safety, visit the DOT's Office of Pipeline Safety.

A few of the safety precautions associated with natural gas pipelines include:

- **Aerial Patrols**—Planes are used to ensure no construction activities are taking place too close to the route of the pipeline, particularly in residential areas. Unauthorized construction and digging is the primary threat to pipeline safety, according to INGAA.
- **Leak Detection**—Natural gas detecting equipment is periodically used by pipeline personnel on the surface to

check for leaks. This is especially important in areas where the natural gas is not odorized.

- **Pipeline Markers**—Signs on the surface above natural gas pipelines indicate the presence of underground pipelines to the public, to reduce the chance of any interference with the pipeline.
- **Gas Sampling**—Routine sampling of the natural gas in pipelines ensures its quality, and may also indicate corrosion of the interior of the pipeline, or the influx of contaminants.
- **Preventative Maintenance**—This involves the testing of valves and the removal of surface impediments to pipeline inspection.
- **Emergency Response**—Pipeline companies have extensive emergency response teams that train for the possibility of a wide range of potential accidents and emergencies.
- **The One Call Program**—All 50 states have instituted what is known as a "one call" program, which provides excavators, construction crews, and anyone interested in digging into the ground around a pipeline with a single phone number that may be called when any excavation activity is planned. This call alerts the pipeline company, which may flag the area, or even send representatives to monitor the digging. The national 3-digit number for one call is "811."

While large interstate natural gas pipelines transport natural gas from the processing regions to the consuming regions and may serve large wholesale users such as industrial or power generation customers directly, it is the distribution system that actually delivers natural gas to most retail customers, including residential natural gas users.

2

Will the Dakota Access Pipeline Threaten Water Supplies?

Aleszu Bajak

Aleszu Bajak is a senior writer for the Cross Sections blog and his science journalism has appeared in various sites such as The Washington Post, Science, and Nature. Bajak teaches at Northeastern University and Brandeis University, and in 2013 completed a fellowship at M.I.T.

Supporters of the Dakota Access Pipeline insist that it is needed to transport crude oil from North Dakota to existing pipelines. It is a fact that consumers in the U.S. use large amounts of fuel every day and the oil from North Dakota would help meet this demand. But, as the following piece by Aleszu Bajak reveals, detractors worry that the Dakota Access Pipeline could rupture, causing spills that would threaten water supplies from the Missouri River.

In what has been described as one of the largest gatherings of tribal representatives in history, thousands of supporters have joined local members of the Standing Rock Sioux and hundreds of other Native American nations over the last several months in an attempt to block the Dakota Access Pipeline. The $3.7 billion conduit would transport crude oil from North Dakota's booming

"The Dakota Access Pipeline Fight Has Once Again Put The Nation's Oil Pipeline Infrastructure in the Spotlight. It's Old, New, Safe, and Worrisome," by Aleszu Bajak, Undark, December 9, 2016. Reprinted by Permission.

Bakken shale-oil region, through South Dakota and Iowa, and onward to Illinois, where it would connect with existing pipelines.

At issue: The 1,172-mile pipeline, while viewed by supporters as an economic boon, would abut sacred tribal lands and come uncomfortably close to precious water resources. After weeks of sometimes violent confrontations with police and federal officials, those concerns seemed to prevail, with the Obama administration announcing over the weekend that it would not allow the final stretch of the Dakota Access pipeline to cross the Missouri River at Lake Oahe in North Dakota. Instead, the administration called for a full environmental review and an exploration of alternative routes.

Crowds cheered on Sunday as the news broke, but with the pipeline nearly complete—and a pro-oil Donald Trump just weeks away from inauguration as the nation's new president—the latest decision may have little impact on the project's ultimate completion.

Whatever the final outcome—and aside from real and pressing issues like tribal rights, or whether, given the imperatives of climate change, additional fossil fuel infrastructure is a smart move—the battle over the Dakota Access project, like the infamous Keystone XL fight before it, also raises a simple question: How safe are modern oil pipelines, and are there better ways to move crude?

Over 70,000 miles of crude oil pipelines—most of them underground—spread like vasculature beneath the earthen skin of the United States. Those conduits, sometimes wide enough for a person to shimmy through, transport around one billion gallons of oil every day from production fields to refineries, and they help to satisfy the nation's oil habit, which amounts to about 19.4 million barrels (or 814 million gallons) of oil consumed every day, on average. But with that much oil and that much pipe—enough to circle the globe nearly three times—accidents are inevitable. In fact, since 2010, there have been more than 1,300 crude oil spills in the United States, according to data collected by the Pipeline and Hazardous Materials Safety Administration, a regulatory arm of the U.S. Department of Transportation.

That's one crude oil spill every other day.

According to PHMSA, most of these incidents are contained by pipeline operators, and the majority of the spilled oil is recovered. Of the 8.9 million gallons spilled since 2010, the agency has reported that over 70 percent, or 6.3 million gallons, has been recovered. Filtering PHMSA data to look at spills in onshore water crossings only, like rivers, however, the recovery rate drops to just 30 percent. Underwater or elsewhere, small leaks and ruptures can go (and have gone) unnoticed for days—even weeks—before companies manage to detect the problem and shut the pipeline down.

In the meantime, that underground seepage can quickly reach devastating volumes. Rivers contaminated by oil spills can take sometimes take years and hundreds of millions of dollars to remediate. And despite intensive cleanup efforts, the presence of spilled hydrocarbons can sometimes persist in soil and aquifers for decades.

Crude oil courses through pipelines at astonishingly high pressures—sometimes at more than 1,000 pounds per square inch, equal to the pressure felt more than 2,300 feet underwater. What may start as a small leak brought on by corrosion or negligent maintenance can end up spilling hundreds of thousands of gallons of poisonous crude oil and its accompanying chemical lubricants into fields, rivers and aquifers with breathtaking speed. That's in spite of carbon steel pipes and reinforced walls that can reach almost one inch in thickness.

Making matters worse, aging pipeline, much of it built of wrought iron and bare steel, is especially vulnerable to the elements. About 45 percent of all crude oil pipeline in the United States—more than 30,000 miles—was installed before 1970. About 7,000 miles are made of pipe that was laid before World War II. "This is where corrosion rears its ugly head," says Paul Bommer, a senior lecturer in the department of petroleum and geosystems engineering at the University of Texas at Austin. "Corrosion nibbles away at the thickness of the pipe until finally the pipe isn't thick enough and it doesn't matter what the strength of the steel is anymore."

"When the hole finally gets deep enough, it'll get a leak," Bommer continues. "With 1,000 psi, you can push a lot of fluid through a small diameter hole and probably nobody notices until it starts bubbling up in someone's field."

In 2013, that's exactly what happened in Tioga, North Dakota, when a wheat farmer's combine tires became coated in crude more than a week after an underground pipeline sprang a leak from a dime-sized hole in a 6-inch pipe. In all, about 870,000 gallons of crude were spilled. Tesoro Logistics, the pipeline operator responsible for cleaning up the spill, spent $42 million and two years mopping up and processing the contaminated soil.

Three years earlier, a crude oil pipeline ruptured along a problematic section of pipe and spilled 843,000-gallons into a tributary of the Kalamazoo River in Marshall, Michigan. That eventually became the most expensive on-shore spill in U.S. history, costing Canadian pipeline operator Enbridge $1.2 billion in clean-up and environmental restoration. An investigation by the National Transportation Safety Board found that an 80-inch gash had gone unnoticed by the pipeline control center for full day. For 17 hours, Enbridge continued feeding oil into the leaky line.

The possibility of a similar rupture occurring at some point along the new Dakota Access Pipeline is what had many protesters flowing to North Dakota in an attempt to block, or at least re-route, that pipeline. Critics of the Dakota Access project have called for a reevaluation of the pipeline's proposed trajectory, arguing that developers did not sufficiently consider its environmental impacts. Chief among the questions: How would a spill play out if the pipeline began leaking at one of its many river crossings? The conduit, which would move almost 20 million gallons of crude oil per day at 1,440 psi through pipe with walls less than an inch thick (the range is between 0.429 and 0.625 inches thick, according to Energy Transfer Partners, the company building the pipeline), could foul key agricultural and drinking water resources for the Standing Rock Sioux tribe and others.

The most sensitive water crossing in this regard is undoubtedly the Missouri River, and at some point in North Dakota, if the project is to complete the link from the Bakken to the Midwest, the pipeline will need to cross it. Under normal circumstances, and like most pipelines, the Dakota Access pipeline has been laid, link by link, into excavated trenches, and then buried under at least three feet of soil. Where the pipeline must slip under more sensitive features—crop land, highways, rivers—it is tunneled much deeper.

In breaching the Missouri, Energy Transfer partners had planned to bore a tunnel some 7,800 feet long underneath a reservoir along the river known as Lake Oahe. Federal guidelines require pipelines to be at least 3 feet below the natural bottom of water sources that are less than 12 feet deep, but the Dakota pipeline would run far deeper, says Michael Rosenfeld, chief engineer with Kiefner and Associates, a technical services provider to the pipeline industry. That's because engineers use horizontal directional drilling—the same technology that has helped to unlock vast amounts of deep shale oil and gas in the first place—to carve a long, gently sloping tunnel beneath those surface features being avoided. Once the bore hole is complete, a pre-welded and pre-inspected section of high-yield strength steel pipe is then threaded through and connected to the rest of the pipeline.

"You may be 40 feet under the river or the highway and it's a continuously curved path," says Rosenfeld, explaining how long and deep the tunnel must be to allow for a slight bend in the large-diameter steel pipeline. That also means that pipelines typically make their deeper dive underground a significant distance from the feature they are slipping under—and that depth and distance could be a silver lining, Rosenfeld says, as they can help protect both the resource being avoided, and the pipeline itself. "It does wind up typically being installed fairly deep which generally is to its benefit because rivers can flood or erode their banks and this keeps the pipe well away from areas where it can get exposed to those kinds of natural processes."

Drawings submitted to the federal government as part of the Dakota Access project's environmental impact assessment suggest that the pipeline would be anywhere from 92 feet to as much as 117 feet beneath the nominal bottom of the Oahe reservoir.

Of course, for all of this technical derring-do, underwater geography is constantly in flux, and oil leaks have been known to spring from pipelines nominally buried deep under river bottoms—often with disastrous results. A pipeline that slipped some 8 feet below the bottom of the Yellowstone River, for example, was found to be fully exposed on the riverbed and leaking thousands of gallons of oil—just a few years later. In recent years, oil has seeped up from pipelines beneath wetlands near the Kalamazoo, and underneath culverts built for caribou crossings in Alaska.

Just this week, a "significant" pipeline leak was found to be spilling oil into a tributary of the Little Missouri River near Belfield, North Dakota. "The incident was reported by a landowner who saw oil leaking from the 6-inch pipeline into the creek," The *Grand Forks Herald* newspaper noted.

For its part, Dakota Access, LLC, a subsidiary of Energy Transfer Partners, says it's employing the latest technology to inspect and periodically monitor the Dakota Access conduit—and that these safety measures mean an oil spill into the Missouri River is improbable. "The depth of the pipeline below the respective rivers … and the design and operation measures that meet or exceed the respective Pipeline and Hazardous Materials Safety Administration (PHMSA) regulations make a release into either waterbody very unlikely to occur," the company declared in an environmental assessment.

Matthew Horn, a senior scientist with RPS Group, a consultancy firm that performs risk assessments and spill modelling for pipeline projects, including the Dakota Access, repeated that assessment in a phone call. With the pipeline dozens of feet below layers of sand, clay, and rock, the earth would act to slow the movement of oil should a leak occur, giving responders time to detect and address the problem. "If you're 92 feet below a river and we're talking about maybe a barrel of oil a day, that's not going to transport anywhere quickly," Horn said. "It's not as though you'll have a leak and see a giant oil slick on the river right away."

A burst weld or a full bore rupture, on the other hand, would send oil "tens of kilometers down the river," Horn said.

Spill and environmental risk models for the Dakota Access project's proposed Lake Oahe crossing were submitted as part of the environmental assessment required by federal law. But as noted by Jo-Ellen Darcy, the Assistant Secretary of the Army (Civil Works) who issued the decision to halt the project last weekend, those spill models have been withheld from the public "because of security and sensitivities."

Representatives of Energy Transfer Partners and Dakota Access LLC did not respond to requests for comment on the safety of its pipeline, or on the recent Obama administration to reconsider its route under the Missouri. But a public relations specialist representing the company, Lisa Dillinger, provided a fact-sheet outlining the various safety measures it intends to employ once the pipeline begins operating. These include: aerial and ground inspections every two weeks; "24/7 monitoring" from a control center with the ability to shut down the pipeline remotely or in person; and the use of a so-called Advanced Supervisory Control and Data Acquisition system "to constantly monitor sensing devices placed along the pipeline to track pressure, temperature, density, and flow."

In addition to those measures, federal law requires the operator inspect the pipeline every five years using "smart pigs," tools that move through the pipe and measure indentations, buckles or evidence of corrosion in the pipe. Shut-off valves before and after the river crossing are also required by law, Rosenfeld notes. "There have to be shut-off valves on the upstream side and backflow check valves on the downstream side to protect that waterway," he says.

In the case of an oil spill, those valves can be shut off remotely—from as far away as Houston, Rosenfeld says.

Many regulatory reform advocates would like to see more frequent pigging than every five years, and not everyone has faith in other established safety regimes—even if they are enshrined in federal code. Should oil reach the Missouri River or another body of water, drinking water intakes would be threatened. It's a worst-case scenario that many parties have raised, including the Environmental Protection Agency, in a letter dated March 11:

"Our experience in spill response indicates that a break or leak in oil pipelines can result in significant impacts to water resources. We note the capacity of the proposed DAPL is 13,100 to 16,600 gallons per minute of crude oil. Despite the expectation of a low probability of a significant spill reaching the Missouri River and lakes, the proposed Missouri River crossings are located 10 miles above the Fort Yates and 15-20 miles above the Williston, North Dakota, drinking water intakes. There would be very little time to determine if a spill or leak affecting surface waters is occurring, to notify water treatment plants and to have treatment plant staff on site to shut down the water intakes."

The Standing Rock Sioux tribe plans to move to a new water intake roughly 70 miles downstream from the pipeline crossing as early as next year. That might alleviate some of the risk, but concerns over the Oahe crossing have continued to mount. A pipeline safety consultancy hired by opponents of the Dakota Access project suggested just last month, for example, that the U.S. Army Corps of Engineers had likely underestimated the potential for the new crude oil pipeline to spill into the Missouri River—and overstated the ability of operators to identify major spills.

Energy Transfer defended the Army Corps analysis, and insisted that the environmental concerns attending the pipeline had been "adequately addressed."

That sort of back-and-forth is not all that surprising, given the stakeholders on all sides, but it's worth noting that, while disasters have happened, pipelines overall have a relatively clean track record. The overwhelming majority of the 350 billion gallons of crude oil transported every year in the U.S. reaches its destination.

Of course, no two oil spills are the same and environmental remediation efforts can take years, as the impacts of residual chemicals on natural resources like land, water, and wildlife linger. The larger the spill, the longer lasting the effects and the deeper the environmental harm, which can range from wildlife mortality to long-term health effects in humans, including spill cleanup workers.

Still, according to Sarah Stafford, a professor of economics at William & Mary who has studied pipelines and government regulation, the alternatives to pipelines are far more worrisome. "For all the problems that pipelines have, they're probably the safest means of transport," Stafford says. "It's better that it's in a pipeline than in a railcar or on a highway."

That, of course, is an argument that has been made many times in the past—and it's one that environmental advocates call a red herring. During the fight over the Keystone XL pipeline, for example, the Natural Resources Defense Council, the Washington D.C.-based environmental advocacy group, argued that the construction of pipelines would do nothing to stop the disasters associated with transporting crude oil by train, because oil companies were still keen on using both modes of transport.

Advocates say the same is true with the Dakota Access project. "You have to look at the economics of North Dakota," says Jesse Coleman, a researcher with Greenpeace's U.S. investigations team. "They're already getting it out by rails and they will continue to. They're not going to stop using the rail system because they built this pipeline."

While crude oil shipments by rail are down nationwide compared to the same time last year, North Dakota is still booming: "The Bakken region has accounted for the vast majority of rail crude oil originations in recent years," according to a November 2015 report from the Association of American Railroads. Completion of the Dakota Access Pipeline may affect rail traffic, but it won't stop it in its tracks, predicts Coleman. And unless

Americans lose their appetite for fossil fuels, the country's extensive web of crude oil superhighways will keep humming along.

"Until the day comes that people aren't using the volume of fuel that we use day in and day out, there's no other way," said Bommer, the University of Texas engineer. "Those pipelines, we can't do without them."

3

Negative Effects Outweigh Benefits of Keystone XL Pipeline

Melissa Denchak

Melissa Denchak is an author and freelance editor based in Brooklyn, New York who writes for various publications and organizations—including the Natural Resources Defense Council.

The controversial Keystone XL Pipeline would be used to transport tar sands oil from Alberta, Canada to the Gulf Coast of Texas. Writer Melissa Denchak breaks down the various controversies attached to the project in the following viewpoint. Critics claim this thick, corrosive oil would cause more pipeline leaks and corresponding environmental problems. Supporters claim that KXL would provide jobs, lower gas prices, and national energy security.

I f ever there was an environmental battle exemplifying a game of ping pong, it would be the stop-start story of the Keystone XL pipeline, also known as KXL. From the time it was proposed in 2008, through seven years of dogged citizen protest and various conflicting legislative orders by the federal government, the path for this controversial oil pipeline has never been smooth. In the most recent chapter of the fight, President Obama vetoed the pipeline in November 2015—acknowledging its pervasive threats to ecosystems, drinking water sources, and public health; and

"What Is the Keystone Pipeline?" by Melissa Denchak, Natural Resources Defense Council, April 7, 2017. Included with permission from the Natural Resources Defense Council.

advancing a national commitment to decreasing our reliance on dirty energy. Then, immediately after taking office, President Trump reversed course on Obama's pledge. In January, he signed an executive order to advance Keystone XL (as well as the Dakota Access Pipeline, and in March, the U.S. State Department issued the pipeline developers their long-sought cross-border permit, reversing course on the department's own previous decision, claiming the project would now "support U.S. priorities relating to energy security, economic development, and infrastructure." Here's an overview of the export tar sands pipeline that's become one of the foremost climate controversies of our time.

What is Keystone XL?

The Keystone XL pipeline extension, proposed by energy infrastructure company TransCanada in 2008, was designed to transport the planet's dirtiest fossil fuel to market, fast. An expansion of the company's existing Keystone Pipeline System, operating since 2008 (and already sending Canadian crude from Alberta to various processing hubs in the middle of the United States), it would dramatically increase capacity to process the 168 billion barrels of crude oil locked up in Canada's boreal forest. To be precise, it would transport 830,000 barrels of Alberta tar sands oil per day to refineries on the Gulf Coast of Texas.

Some 2.6 million miles of oil and gas pipelines already run through our country. But Keystone XL wouldn't be your average pipeline, and tar sands aren't your average crude.

Keystone and Tar Sands

Beneath the wilds of northern Alberta's boreal forest is a sludgy, sticky deposit called tar sands. These sands contain bitumen, a gooey type of petroleum that can be converted into fuel. It's no small feat extracting oil from tar sands, and doing so comes with steep environmental and economic costs. Nevertheless, in the mid-2000s, with gas prices on the rise, oil companies ramped up production and sought additional ways to move their product from Canada's remote tar sands fields to midwestern and Gulf Coast refineries.

Keystone Pipeline Map

The Keystone extension actually comprises two segments. The first, a southern leg, has already been completed and runs between Cushing, Oklahoma, and Port Arthur, Texas. Opponents of this project—now called the Gulf Coast Pipeline—say that TransCanada took advantage of legal loopholes to push the pipeline through, securing a U.S. Army Corps of Engineers permit and dodging the Environmental Protection Agency's more rigorous vetting process, which requires public input. The second segment is the currently contested 1,179-mile northern leg—a shortcut of sorts—that would run from Hardisty, Alberta, through Montana and South Dakota to Steele City, Nebraska.

Following a rigorous, robust analysis with substantial public engagement, President Obama declined to grant the northern leg of the Keystone XL project the U.S. State Department Presidential Permit required to construct, maintain, and operate a pipeline across a United States border. Though President Trump has since granted this permit and removed this barrier to its construction, significant legal, regulatory and economic barriers remain for the pipeline to become operational.

Keystone Pipeline Environmental Impact

Leaks and the pipeline

Tar sands oil is thicker, more acidic, and more corrosive than lighter conventional crude, and this ups the likelihood that a pipeline carrying it will leak. Indeed, one study found that between 2007 and 2010, pipelines moving tar sands oil in Midwestern states spilled three times more per mile than the U.S. national average for pipelines carrying conventional crude. Within its first year of operation, TransCanada's original Keystone Pipeline System leaked 12 times; one incident in North Dakota sent a 60-foot, 21,000-gallon geyser of tar sands oil spewing into the air.

Complicating matters, leaks can be difficult to detect. And when tar sands oil does spill, it's highly volatile—posing an elevated risk of explosion—and more difficult to clean up than conventional crude. People and wildlife coming into contact with tar sands oil are exposed to toxic chemicals, and rivers and wetland environments are at particular risk from a spill. "It immediately sinks to the bottom" of the waterway, says NRDC staff attorney Kim Ong, "and there is, to date, no known way of cleaning up this oil." (For evidence, recall the 2010 tar sands oil spill in Kalamazoo, Michigan, a disaster that cost Enbridge more than a billion dollars in cleanup fees and took six years to settle in court.) Keystone XL would cross agriculturally important and environmentally sensitive areas, including more than 1,000 rivers, streams, aquifers and water bodies. One is Nebraska's Ogallala Aquifer, which provides drinking water for millions as well as 30 percent of America's irrigation water. A spill would be devastating to the farms, ranches, and communities that depend on these crucial ecosystems.

What is tar sands oil?
The tar sands industry is just as hard on the cradle of its business. Its mines are a blight on Canada's boreal, where operations dig up and flatten forests to access the oil below, destroying wildlife habitat. They deplete and pollute freshwater resources, create massive ponds of toxic waste, and threaten the health and livelihood of the First Nations people who live near them. Refining the sticky black gunk produces piles of petroleum coke, a hazardous by-product. What's more, the whole process of getting the oil out and making it usable creates three to four times the carbon pollution of conventional crude extraction and processing. "This isn't your grandfather's typical oil," says Danielle Droitsch, senior policy analyst for NRDC's Canada project. "It's nasty stuff."

Keystone and climate change

A fully realized Keystone XL would lead to more mining of that "nasty stuff" by accelerating the pace at which it's produced and transported. (Indeed, Keystone XL was viewed as a necessary ingredient in the oil industry's plans to triple tar sands production by 2030.)

It would also lead to greater greenhouse gas emissions. In 2014, the U.S. Environmental Protection Agency stated that tar sands oil emits 17 percent more carbon than other types of crude, but ironically, the State Department revised this number upward three years later, stating that the emissions could be "5 percent to 20 percent higher than previously indicated." That means burdening the planet with an extra 177 million metric tons of greenhouse gas emissions annually, the same impact as adding 37 million passenger vehicles to the road. Finally, the pipeline would undermine efforts to prioritize clean energy like wind and solar and to minimize global warming. Leading climate scientist and former NASA researcher James Hansen has warned that fully exploiting Canada's tar sands reserves would mean "game over" for our climate. In short, tar sands oil represents no small threat to our environment, and our best stance against it, as the rallying cry goes, is to "keep it in the ground."

Keystone Pipeline Controversy

Opposition to Keystone XL centers on the devastating environmental consequences of the project. The pipeline has faced years of sustained protests from environmental activists and organizations; indigenous communities; religious leaders; and farmers, ranchers, and business owners along its proposed route. One such protest, a historic act of civil disobedience outside the White House in August 2011, resulted in the arrest of more than 1,200 demonstrators. More than 90 leading scientists and economists have opposed the project, in addition to unions and world leaders such as the Dalai Lama, Archbishop Desmond Tutu, and former president Jimmy Carter (together, these and other Nobel laureates have written letters against the project). In 2014 more than two million comments urging a rejection of the pipeline were submitted to the State Department during a 30-day public comment period.

In the two years leading up to the November 2014 midterm elections, the fossil fuel industry spent more than $720 million to court allies in Congress. When industry-friendly politicians took charge of both congressional houses in January 2015, their first order of business was to pass a bill to speed up approval of Keystone XL. (That effort failed.)

"So what if there's no pipeline . . . Big Oil will find a way."

One of the central arguments by pipeline pushers is that tar sands expansion will move forward with or without Keystone XL. This has proved to be untrue. Dealing in tar sands oil is an expensive endeavor. It's costly both to produce and to ship, particularly by rail, which would be an alternative to Keystone XL. Indeed, moving crude by rail to the Gulf costs twice as much as by pipe. For companies considering whether to invest in a long-lived tar sands project (which could last for 50 years), access to cheap pipeline capacity will play a major role in the decision to move forward or not. Without Keystone XL, the tar sands industry has canceled projects rather than shift to rail, subsequently leaving more of the earth's dirtiest fuel in the ground where it belongs.

Keystone Pipeline Economic Facts

Will the pipeline create jobs?
The oil industry has lobbied hard to get KXL built by using false claims, political arm-twisting, and big bucks. When TransCananda said the pipeline would create nearly 119,000 jobs, a State Department report concluded only 3,900 temporary construction jobs would appear and that the number of permanent jobs would hover around 35.

Will the pipeline lower gas prices?
Dirty energy lobbyists claimed developing tar sands would protect our national energy security and bring U.S. fuel prices down. But NRDC and its partners found the majority of Keystone XL oil would be sent to markets overseas (aided by the recent reversal of a ban on crude oil exports)—and could even lead to higher prices at the pump.

President Trump and the Keystone Pipeline

When President Obama refused to grant the presidential permit necessary to build TransCanada's Keystone XL oil pipeline in November 2015, he struck a blow against polluting powers and acknowledged the consensus on this misguided project from a wide swath of people and organizations. "America is now a global leader when it comes to taking serious action to fight climate change," he said. "And, frankly, approving this project would have undercut that global leadership." Obama's decision echoed a seven-year State Department review process with EPA input that concluded the pipeline would fail to serve national interests.

Upon sweeping into office, President Trump—with his pro-polluter cabinet of fossil fuel advocates, billionaires, and bankers—quickly demonstrated that his priorities differ. On his fourth day in office, Trump signed an executive order that allows Keystone XL to move forward. On March 28, 2017, his administration illegally approved a cross-border permit for the pipeline, reversing the Obama Administration's robust National Interest Determination process.

The opposition has been swift and strong. Within days of the reversal, NRDC and other groups sued the Trump Administration, contending that the State Department acted in violation of the National Environmental Policy Act and the Administrative Procedure Act by relying on an outdated and incomplete environmental impact analysis and by arbitrarily reversing its earlier decision.

Hurdles Remaining in Keystone XL's Path

The Trump administration still faces numerous hurdles in its attempt to fast-track Keystone XL. For starters, the process must still meet the requirements of federal environmental law, which require objective consideration of the environmental impacts of the pipeline. Federal Clean Water Act permits are also still required. In Nebraska, a long and contentious opposition to routing the pipeline continues, and in-state opposition is in fact growing. TransCanada must seek approval from Nebraskan authorities—a process that can take 8 to 12 months, and then must still seek right-of-way access for the pipeline. Ranchers and Native Americans are ready to fight to protect the lands they have stewarded for generations.

Finally, even as Trump and TransCanada try to revive the pipeline, polls show that a majority of Americans now oppose it and the market case has also deteriorated. Low oil prices and increasing public concern over the climate have led Shell, Exxon, Statoil and Total to either sell their tar sands assets or write them down. Because of this growing market recognition, major new tar sands projects haven't been approved for years.

As NRDC President Rhea Suh said prior to President Trump's inauguration, "Whatever we voted on in November [2016], nobody voted for dirty water and air. Nobody voted to walk away from climate leadership and millions of clean energy jobs. And nobody voted to hand over our country to a pollute-ocracy that puts polluter profits first—and puts the rest of us at risk."

4

Delivering Natural Gas to the Consumer

NaturalGas.org

NaturalGas.org is an educational website designed to educate students, teachers, industry members, government personnel, and the media about the many aspects of the natural gas industry.

Natural gas is delivered to consumers through two million miles of small-diameter distribution pipe throughout the U.S. via their local gas utility. In the following informative piece, readers will learn that many safety measures are employed—including the addition of a chemical to the normally odorless natural gas. The "rotten egg smell" then allows professionals and consumers to detect gas leaks.

Distribution is the final step in delivering natural gas to customers. While some large industrial, commercial, and electric generation customers receive natural gas directly from high capacity interstate and intrastate pipelines (usually contracted through natural gas marketing companies), most other users receive natural gas from their local gas utility, also called a local distribution company (LDC). LDCs are regulated utilities involved in the delivery of natural gas to consumers within a specific geographic area. There are two basic types of natural gas utilities: those owned by investors, and public gas systems owned by local governments.

"Natural Gas Distribution," by NaturalGas.org, September 20, 2013. Reprinted by Permission.

Local distribution companies typically transport natural gas from delivery points located on interstate and intrastate pipelines to households and businesses through thousands of miles of small-diameter distribution pipe. The delivery point where the natural gas is transferred from a transmission pipeline to the local gas utility is often termed the "citygate," and is an important market center for the pricing of natural gas in large urban areas. Typically, Utilities take ownership of the natural gas at the citygate, and deliver it to each individual customer's meter. This requires an extensive network of small-diameter distribution pipe. The U.S. Department of Transportation's Pipeline and Hazardous Materials Safety Administration reports that there are just over 2 million miles of distribution pipe in the U.S., including city mains and service pipelines that connect each meter to the main.

Because of the transportation infrastructure required to move natural gas to many diverse customers across a reasonably wide geographic area, distribution costs typically make up about half of natural gas costs for households and small volume customers. While large pipelines can reduce unit costs by transmitting large volumes of natural gas, distribution companies must deliver relatively small volumes to many more different locations. According to the Energy Information Administration (EIA), transmission and distribution costs represented about half of a typical residential natural gas customer's monthly gas utility bill in 2009, with costs of the physical natural gas commodity itself representing the other half.

Delivery of Natural Gas

The delivery of natural gas to its point of end use by a distribution utility is much like the transportation of natural gas discussed in the transportation section. However, distribution involves moving smaller volumes of gas at much lower pressures over shorter distances to a great number of individual users. Smaller-diameter pipe also is used to transport natural gas from the citygate to individual consumers.

The natural gas is periodically compressed to ensure pipeline flow, although local compressor stations are typically smaller than those used for interstate transportation. Because of the smaller volumes of natural gas to be moved, as well as the small-diameter pipe that is used, the pressure required to move natural gas through the distribution network is much lower than that found in the transmission pipelines. While natural gas traveling through interstate pipelines may be compressed to as much as 1,500 pounds per square inch (psi), natural gas traveling through the distribution network requires as little as 3 psi of pressurization and is as low as ¼ psi at the customer's meter. The natural gas to be distributed is typically depressurized at or near the citygate, as well as scrubbed and filtered (even though it has already been processed prior to distribution through interstate pipelines) to ensure low moisture and particulate content. In addition, mercaptan—the source of the familiar rotten egg smell in natural gas—is added by the utility prior to distribution. This is added because natural gas is odorless and colorless, and the familiar odor of mercaptan makes the detection of leaks much easier.

Traditionally, rigid steel pipe was used to construct distribution networks. However, new technology is allowing the use of flexible plastic and corrugated stainless steel tubing in place of rigid steel pipe. These new types of tubing allow cost reduction, installation flexibility and easier repairs for both local distribution companies and natural gas consumers.

Another innovation in the distribution of natural gas is the use of electronic meter-reading systems. The natural gas that is consumed by any one customer is measured by on-site meters, which essentially keep track of the volume of natural gas consumed at that location. Traditionally, in order to bill customers correctly, meter-reading personnel had to be dispatched to record these volumes. However, new electronic meter-reading systems are capable of transmitting this information directly to the utility. This results in cost savings for the utility, which are in turn passed along to customers.

The installation of natural gas distribution pipe requires the same process as for larger pipelines: the excavation of trenches into which the pipe is laid. However, new trenching techniques are allowing for the installation of distribution pipe with less impact on the above ground surroundings. Guided drilling systems are used to excavate an underground hole in which the pipe may be inserted, and can lead to significant excavation and restoration savings. This is particularly important in crowded urban settings and scenic rural environments, where the installation of natural gas distribution pipe can be a major inconvenience for residents and business owners.

Supervisory control and data acquisition (SCADA) systems, similar to those used by large pipeline companies, are also used by local distribution companies. These systems can integrate gas flow control and measurement with other accounting, billing, and contract systems to provide a comprehensive measurement and control system for the local gas utility. This allows accurate, timely information on the status of the distribution network to be used by the utility, to ensure efficient and effective service at all times.

Regulation of Natural Gas Distribution

Traditionally, local gas utilities have been awarded exclusive rights to distribute natural gas in a specified geographic area, as well as perform services like billing, safety inspection, and providing natural gas hookups for new customers. Like interstate pipelines, utilities have historically been viewed as natural monopolies. Because of the high cost of constructing the distribution infrastructure, it is uneconomic to lay multiple redundant distribution networks in any one area, resulting in only one utility offering distribution services. Because of their position as natural monopolies in a given geographic area, distribution companies have historically been regulated to ensure that monopoly power is not abused, and natural gas consumers do not fall victim to overly high distribution costs or inefficient delivery systems.

State public utility commissions are charged with the oversight and regulation of investor owned local natural gas utilities. Those utilities owned by local governments are typically governed by local government agencies to ensure that the needs and preferences of customers are met in a cost effective manner. State regulation of local distribution companies has a variety of objectives, including ensuring adequate supply, dependable service, and reasonable prices for consumers, while also allowing for an adequate rate of return for investor owned Utilities. State regulators are also responsible for overseeing the construction of new distribution networks, including approving installation sites and proposed additions to the network. Regulatory orders and methods of oversight vary from state to state. To learn more about the regulation of natural gas distribution in your state, visit the National Association of Regulatory Utility Commissioners (NARUC).

Historically, local distribution companies offered only "bundled" services; that is, they combined the cost of transportation, distribution, and the natural gas itself into one price for consumers. However, beginning in the 1990s, residential "customer choice" programs began to be offered as part of a movement toward the retail "unbundling" of natural gas sales. Many states now offer programs in which customers may choose a supplier from whom to purchase the natural gas commodity separately, and use the gas utility simply for service and delivery of that gas. Customer choice programs are in place in more than 20 states and the District of Columbia. To learn more about the status of state distribution customer choice programs, visit the EIA website.

Although the majority of residential and small commercial customers still tend to purchase "bundled" natural gas from utilities, the increasingly important role of natural gas marketers, as well as the innovation fueled by increasing competition in the marketplace, is leading to innovative ways of supplying natural gas to small volume users as well as new bundled service options, such as home security systems.

Distribution and Safety

Local distribution companies, like the larger interstate and intrastate pipelines, maintain the highest safety standards to ensure that preventable accidents are avoided, and problems with the distribution network are remedied in a timely fashion. Many of the safety programs maintained by utilities are quite similar to those of interstate pipeline companies. Safety measures at the local level include:

- **Leak Detection Equipment**—Utilities have in place sophisticated leak detection equipment, designed to pick up on leaks of natural gas from the distribution network. Utilities also add odorants to the natural gas to make it easier to detect a leak.
- **Safety Education Programs**—Utilities typically run natural gas safety seminars in schools, community centers, and through other organizations to ensure customers are well versed in natural gas safety procedures and know what to do in the event of a leak or emergency.
- **Technicians on Call**—Utilities maintain fleets of technicians on call 24 hours a day, seven days a week to respond to customers' problems and concerns.
- **Emergency Preparedness**—Utilities participate in community and local emergency preparedness programs, educating and preparing for emergency events such as natural disasters.
- **One Call Systems**—Provides customers, contractors, and excavators with a single phone number to call before commencing excavation or construction, to ensure that the pipelines, and other buried facilities are not damaged. A national "call-before-you-dig" phone number of "811" was adopted in 2008 with the support of utilities, communities, emergency responders and government officials.

These are but a few of the safety measures maintained by local distribution companies. Especially important for the safe distribution of natural gas, particularly in densely populated areas, is the education of customers. By teaching natural gas users the safe use of natural gas, what to do in an emergency, and how to detect leaks, distribution companies ensure that the distribution of natural gas will remain one of the safest forms of energy transmission. For more information on natural gas safety in your area, contact your natural gas utility. For information on natural gas pipelines, please visit the Department of Transportation's Office of Pipeline Safety.

5

All Methods of Oil Transport Have Risks and Benefits

Juliana Henao

As a communications intern, Juliana Henao wrote about pipelines and oil trains for FracTracker Alliance. She has a Master's degree in Environmental Science and Management from Duquesne University.

Since the proposal for the Keystone XL pipeline, media reporting has been focused on incidents of pipeline leaks and spills, along with oil train incidents. Data supports this information and concludes that every method of oil transportation brings both risk and benefit. In the viewpoint below from environmental science writer Juliana Henao, a possible alternative is suggested: that of safer energy sources such as solar.

Media outlets have been very focused recently on reporting oil train derailments and explosions. Additionally, the Keystone XL pipeline has hastened political debates and arguments for years by both political parties since its initial proposal in 2008—and the May 19th pipeline oil spill in California isn't helping matters. In the midst of all of this commotion, a million questions are being asked, yet no one can seem to reach a conclusion about what method of transporting oil is truly safest and economically feasible—or if we are just stuck between a rock and a hard place.

"Pipelines vs Oil Trains," by Juliana Henao, FracTracker Alliance, May 26, 2015. Reprinted by Permission. FracTracker Alliance: FracTracker.org, May 2015.

Some say the solution to this problem is transporting the volatile crude via pipelines, while others believe it is a matter of increasing regulations, standards, and compliance for transport by train. The answer is simply not simple.

In light of this, a few of the folks at FracTracker gathered some facts on pipelines vs oil trains to lay out this issue in a clearer fashion.

Let's start with trains.

Benefits

Due to the increasing demand of crude oil supply, there has been increasing activity in the transportation of crude oil by rail, which provides flexibility and quick transportation throughout the U.S. and its 115 refineries. Railroads are also willing to offer shippers shorter contracts than pipelines and other transportation methods, making them a more favorable method of crude oil transportation.

In 2008, U.S. freight trains were delivering somewhere from 9-10,000 carloads of crude oil. In 2013, they delivered roughly 435,560 carloads of crude oil, showing a 20-fold increase in crude oil shipments.

Risks

Oil trains, as well as pipelines, can pose a detrimental risk to communities and public health in the case of an explosion and/ or spill. *Danger Around the Bend* describes in detail the dangers of transporting Bakken Formation crude oil from North Dakota to parts all over the country.

Some of the risks of transporting volatile crude via train have been clearly depicted in the news with announcements of spills, derailments, and explosions in urban and suburban areas, putting many people in harm's way. Despite the decrease in spills between 1996 and 2007, devastating train accidents like the one on July 6, 2013 have raised questions about the safety of transportation by train.

Trains and train tracks in general can be very dangerous, as demonstrated by the deadly Amtrak train derailment in Philadelphia this May. The total number of incidents in 2014, according to the Federal Railroad Administration, sum up to 11,793—with 818 of those being fatal. These fatalities have been linked to a range of possible causes, but the numbers depict the gravity of safety issues within the railroad regulations.

Regulations

When it comes to train safety and regulations, the Federal Railroad Administration (FRA) is in charge. Some of the current efforts to increase the safety of oil trains include safer tank car design, adding braking power, reducing the train speed limits through urban areas and increasing crew size. One of the most important improvements, however, includes an increase in oil spill response, which is managed through the National Oil and Hazardous Substance Contingency Plan.

Now, let's talk pipelines.

As we all know, finishing the Keystone XL pipeline has stirred years of controversy, since this project was initially proposed back in 2008. On January 31, 2014, the U.S. Department of State released the Final Supplemental Environmental Impact Statement (SEIS) of the Keystone XL Pipeline, which would transport up to 830,000 barrels of tar sand oil per day through an 875-mile long pipeline running from Alberta, Canada, to the Gulf Coast area.

The SEIS discussed the impacts that the proposed pipeline would have on the environment and public health based on research, modeling, and analysis. One of the many purposes of the SEIS is to focus on whether the proposed project serves the national interest by comparing the risks to the benefits—discussed in more detail below.

Risks

The current risks associated with pipelines are similar to the risks associated with other modes of transporting oil across the United States. Oil spills are among the highest risks, but with the XL pipeline, it's a more profound risk due to the type of oil being carried: tar sand oil. Tar sand oil, also known as heavy oil, is known for its tedious processing and its many environmental implications. Burning one single barrel of oil produced from Canadian tar sands generally emits 170 pounds of greenhouse gases into the atmosphere. It also requires large amounts of energy and water, much of which cannot be recycled, to separate the oil from the tar sands and transform the oil into a form of petroleum that can be processed by refineries.

According to the final SEIS:

> The proposed project would emit approximately 24 million metric tons of carbon dioxide per year during the construction period (up to three times as much than producing conventional crude), which would be directly emitted through fuel use in construction vehicles and equipment as well as land clearing activities including open burning, and indirectly from electricity usage.

Additional risks associated with the XL pipeline include potential groundwater contamination of major aquifers—particularly the Ogallala Aquifer—as well as deforestation, habitat destruction, and fragmentation.

In the event of an oil spill from the Keystone XL or other pipelines crossing the U.S., the responsibility for who cleans it up does not fall on TransCanada. According to a report from the Natural Resource Defense Council (NRDC), tar sand oils are exempt from paying into the Oil Spill Liability Trust Fund. Amendments that would require TransCanada to pay the 8-cent-per-barrel fee to the fund have not been passed.

Devastating oil spills such as the one in Santa Barbara in mid-May reflect the impact it not only has on wildlife, but on the local culture, especially on those who depend on fisheries and whose lives revolves around surfing in the brisk waters of the Pacific Ocean. 21,000 gallons of crude oil covers roughly 4 miles of Santa Barbara's coast now, extending about 50 yards into the water.

Benefits

Jobs, jobs, jobs. The economic stimulus is one purported advantage to the XL pipeline. During construction, proposed project spending would support approximately 42,100 jobs, directly and indirectly and around $2 billion in earnings throughout the US, according to the final SEIS. Despite different job creation estimates, any number will contribute significantly to the US gross domestic product, associating a huge economic growth with the construction of the proposed XL pipeline. (TransCanada estimates around 13,000 construction jobs and 7,000 manufacturing jobs, which is about 3 times higher than the State Department's estimate.) In addition, the cost of paying for the Keystone XL project ($3.3 billion) would not be placed on the U.S. but on Keystone.

According to the Pipeline and Hazardous Materials Safety Administration (PHSMA), the industry and their operators have reduced the risk of hazardous materials transportation incidents with death or major injury by 4% every 3 years, and since 2002, they have reduced the risk of a pipeline spill with environmental consequences by an average of 5% per year.[1]

Still, there is more work to be done. Safety issues that the pipeline industry is aiming to fix include:

- **Infrastructure:** Repair obsolete pipeline infrastructure through a pipeline integrity management program and investigate new technologies that can detect pipeline risks.
- **Improving human error and safety culture:** Increase the focus on safety beyond compliance standards and evaluate the potential value of safety management systems.
- **Adding secondary containment:** Limit the spread of HAZMAT in the event of a failure in the primary container, and improve leak detection.

- **Transparency:** Increasing transparency for companies and their accountability.

Moving Forward

All methods of transporting oil present various risks and benefits based on the available data. Explaining both sides of this coin allows us to assess each method's impacts on our economy, environment, and public health. Through these assessments, we can make more informed decisions on what truly serves the nation's interests. Oil and gas transport is a dangerous business, but all transportation industries are improving their management programs and increasing their regulations to provide citizens peace of mind and the safety they deserve. In light of ongoing issues, however, some would ask if these risks are even necessary.

For example, the growth of safer energy resources such as solar energy would significantly cut down the risks mentioned above in addition to providing jobs and stimulating the overall economy. According to the Bureau of Labor Statistics and the Solar Foundation, the growth in direct industry jobs for solar has outweighed oil and gas for the past 3 years. In 2014, new jobs created for the solar industry were more than twice the jobs created for the oil and gas industry. Based on 2014's economics, Kepler Cheuvreux stated that all renewables are already more competitive than oil priced at $100 per barrel: This is because renewables have a higher net energy return on capital invested (EROCI).

As a reader and a citizen, it is important to know the pros and cons of the current activities taking place in our country today. We must be aware of loopholes that may be putting our states, cities, or counties into harm's way, as well as recognize alternative energy sources and regulatory oversight that lessen the threats that oil extraction and transport pose to our health and environment.

Footnote
1. These statistics are based from the Census Bureau analysis and Bureau of Transportation Statistics as of July 2012.

6

Energy Technologies Favored by Climate Skeptics Can Reduce Emissions

Ted Nordhaus and Michael Shellenberger

Ted Nordhaus and Michael Shellenberger are co-founders of the Breakthrough Institute, a research institute dedicated to the issues of energy and the environment, and co-authors of An Ecomodernist Manifesto.

Disagreements about climate policy between conservatives and liberals are well known, but, as this viewpoint by energy researchers Nordhaus and Shellenberger reveals, there is a surprising revelation— energy technologies supported by the Right, including nuclear and natural gas have been actually reducing greenhouse gas emissions. Environmental leaders cite Germany as a model for renewables, but the country has seen its carbon emissions rise. Both the Left and the Right need to listen, understand, debate, and make the best decisions for all.

B eyond the bellowing, name-calling, and cherry-picking of data that have become the hallmark of contemporary climate wars lies a paradox: nuclear and gas. The energy technologies favored by the climate-skeptical Right, including Robert Bryce, Steven Hayward, and the Koch brothers, are doing far more to reduce greenhouse gas emissions than the ones favored by the climate-apocalyptic Left. Following the new IPCC report, as both parties

"Climate Skeptics Against Global Warming," by Michael Shellenberger and Ted Nordhaus, The Breakthrough Institute, September 26, 2013. Reprinted by Permission.

spend the next week slugging it out over what the climate science does or does not tell us, we would do well to remember that science cannot tell us what to do. Making decisions in a democracy requires understanding and tolerating, not attacking and demonizing, values, and viewpoints different from our own. Conservatives, whether or not they think of it as climate policy, have important things to say when it comes to energy. Liberals would do well to start listening.

Over the last decade, progressives have successfully painted conservative climate skepticism as the major stumbling block to reducing greenhouse gas emissions. Exxon and the Koch brothers, the story goes, fund conservative think tanks to sow doubt about climate change and block legislative action. As evidence mounts that anthropogenic global warming is underway, conservatives' flight from reason is putting us all at risk.

This week's release of a new United Nations Intergovernmental Panel on Climate Change report opens another front in the climate wars. But beneath the bellowing, name-calling, and cherry-picking of data that have become the hallmark of contemporary climate politics lies a paradox: the energy technologies favored by the climate-skeptical Right are doing far more to reduce greenhouse gas emissions than the ones favored by the climate-apocalyptic Left.

How much more? Max Luke of Breakthrough Institute ran the numbers and found that, since 1950, natural gas and nuclear prevented 36 times more carbon emissions than wind, solar, and geothermal. Nuclear avoided the creation of 28 billion tons of carbon dioxide, natural gas 26 billion, and geothermal, wind, and solar just 1.5 billion.

Environmental leaders who blame "global warming deniers" for preventing emissions reductions point to Germany's move away from nuclear and to renewables. "Germany is the one big country that's taken this crisis seriously," wrote Bill McKibben. Other progressive and green leaders, including Al Gore, Bill Clinton, and Bobby Kennedy, Jr., have held up Germany's "energy turn," the *Energiewende,* as a model for the world.

But for the second year in a row, Germany has seen its coal use and carbon emissions rise—a fact that climate skeptical conservatives have been quick to point out, and liberal environmental advocates have attempted to obfuscate. "Last year, Germany's solar panels produced about 18 terawatt-hours (that's 18 trillion watt-hours) of electricity," noted Robert Bryce from the conservative Manhattan Institute. "And yet, [utility] RWE's new coal plant, which has less than a 10th as much capacity as Germany's solar sector, will, by itself, produce about 16 terawatt-hours of electricity.

Reagan historian Steven Hayward, formerly of the American Enterprise Institute, noted in the conservative *Weekly Standard* earlier this week, "Coal consumption went *up* 3.9 percent in Germany last year. Likewise, German greenhouse gas emissions— the chief object of *Energiewende*—rose in Germany last year, while they fell in the United States."

Emissions fell in the United States thanks largely to a technology loathed by the Left: fracking. From 2007 to 2012, electricity from natural gas increased from 21.6 to 30.4 percent, while electricity from coal declined from 50 to 38 percent—that's light speed in a notoriously slow-changing sector. And yet the Natural Resources Defense Council, Sierra Club, and most other green groups are working to oppose the expansion of natural gas.

Hayward and Bryce are two of the most respected writers on energy and the environment on the Right. Both are highly skeptical that global warming poses a major threat. Both regularly criticize climate scientists and climate models. Both men are regularly attacked by liberal organizations like Media Matters for working for organizations, the American Enterprise Institute and Manhattan Institute, respectively, that have taken money from both Exxon and the Koch brothers. And yet both men are full-throated advocates for what Bryce calls "N2N"—accelerating the transition from coal to natural gas and then to nuclear.

Arguably, the climate-energy paradox is a bigger problem for the Left than the Right. One cannot logically claim that carbon emissions pose a catastrophic threat to human civilization and then oppose the only two technologies capable of immediately and significantly reducing them. And yet this is precisely the position of Al Gore, Bill McKibben, the Sierra Club, NRDC, and the bulk of the environmental movement.

By contrast, there are plenty of good reasons for climate skeptics to support N2N. A diverse portfolio of energy sources that are cheap, abundant, reliable, and increasingly clean is good for the economy and strengthens national security—all the more so in a world where energy demand will likely quadruple by the end of the century.

Why then is there so much climate skepticism on the Right? One obvious reason is that climate science has long been deployed by liberals and environmentalists to argue not only for their preferred energy technologies but also for sweeping new regulatory powers for the federal government and the United Nations.

But here as well, the green agenda hasn't fared well. Those nations that most rapidly reduced the carbon intensity of their economies over the last 40 years did so neither through regulations nor international agreements. Nations like France and Sweden, which President Obama rightly singled out for praise earlier this month, did so by directly deploying nuclear and hydroelectric power. Now the United States is the global climate leader, despite having neither a carbon price nor emissions trading, thanks to 35 years of public-private investment leading to the shale gas revolution. Meanwhile, there is little evidence that caps and carbon taxes have had much impact on emissions anywhere.

In the end, both Left and Right reject a more pragmatic approach to the climate issue out of fear that doing so might conflict with their idealized visions for the future. Conservatives embrace N2N as a laissez-faire outcome of the free market in the face of overwhelming evidence that neither nuclear nor gas would be viable today had it not been for substantial taxpayer support. Progressives seized on global warming as an existential threat to human civilization because they believed it justified a transition to the energy technologies—decentralized renewables—that they have wanted since the sixties.

The Left, in these ways, has been every bit as guilty as the Right of engaging in "post-truth" climate politics. Consider *New Yorker* writer Ryan Lizza's glowing profile of Tom Steyer, the billionaire bankrolling the anti-Keystone campaign. After Lizza suggested that Steyer and his brother Tom might be the Koch brothers of environmentalism, Steyer objects. The difference, he insists, is that while the Koch brothers are after profit, he is trying to save the world.

It is telling that neither Lizza nor his editors felt it necessary to point out that Steyer is a major investor in renewables and stands to profit from his political advocacy as well. Clearly, Steyer is also motivated by green ideology. But it is hard to argue that the Koch brothers haven't been equally motivated by their libertarian ideology. The two have funded libertarian causes since the 1970s and, notably, were among the minority of major energy interests who opposed cap and trade. Fossil energy interests concerned about protecting their profits, including the country's two largest coal utilities, mostly chose to game the proposed emissions trading system rather than oppose it as the Koch brothers did.

As Kathleen Higgins argues in a new essay for *Breakthrough Journal*, it's high time for progressives to get back in touch with the liberal tradition of tolerance, and pluralism. "Progressives seeking to govern and change society," she writes, should attempt to "see the world from the standpoint of their fiercest opponents. Taking multiple perspectives into account might alert us to more sites of possible intervention and prime us for creative formulations of alternative possibilities for concerted responses to our problems."

As Left and Right spend the next week slugging it out over what the climate science does or does not tell us, we would do well to remember that science cannot tell us what to do. Making decisions in a democracy requires understanding and tolerating, not attacking and demonizing, values and viewpoints different from our own.

Conservatives have important things to say when it comes to energy, whether or not they think of it as climate policy. Liberals would do well to start listening.

7

Pipelines Are the Safest Way to Transport Oil and Natural Gas

Diana Furchtgott-Roth

Diana Furchtgott-Roth is a senior fellow at the Manhattan Institute with an expertise in economics and economic policy. An Oxford educated economist, she writes extensively and is the author of Women's Figures: An Illustrated Guide to the Economic Progress of Women in America *from 2012.*

In the United States there are approximately 500,000 miles of petroleum and natural gas pipelines transporting products, and data from the U.S. Department of Transportation prove that pipelines are the safest method of transport. According to the following viewpoint by economist Diana Furchgott-Roth, by analyzing the situation and comparing the incidents of injury or fatalities, it becomes clear that moving energy products by pipeline is safer than using rail, boat, or road.

The Obama administration's decision to delay approval for the construction of TransCanada Inc.'s proposed Keystone XL pipeline was based, in part, on concerns over the safety and reliability of oil and natural gas pipelines. The pipeline is intended to transport oil from Canada to U.S. refiners on the Gulf of Mexico. In announcing his decision, the president called for a full assessment

"Pipelines Are Safest For Transportation of Oil and Gas," by Diana Furchtgott-Roth, Manhattan Institute for Policy Research, June 2013. Reprinted by Permission. Diana Furchtgott-Roth/Manhatttan Institute.

of "the pipeline's impact, especially on the health and safety of the American people."

Pipelines have been used to transport American natural gas or oil, including from Canada to the United States, for three quarters of a century. Almost 500,000 miles of interstate pipeline crisscross America, carrying crude oil, petroleum products, and natural gas. This extensive and operational infrastructure network is heavily regulated by the Department of Transportation, which monitors the very issues central to the Keystone controversy: safety and reliability.

Thus it is possible to answer, based on experience, the question of whether pipeline transport of oil and gas is safe. It is, moreover, possible to compare the record of oil and gas pipelines to that of transport via rail and road. As the major alternative means of fuel shipment, transport by rail and road has been increasing as limitations on pipeline capacity have become manifest (the underlying reason for the Keystone proposal).

A review of safety and accident statistics provided by the U.S. Department of Transportation for the extensive network of existing U.S. pipelines—including many linked to Canada—clearly show that, in addition to enjoying a substantial cost advantage, pipelines result in fewer spillage incidents and personal injuries than road and rail. Americans are more likely to get struck by lightning than to be killed in a pipeline accident.[1]

The question of how to transport oil and gas safely and reliably is not a transitory one linked only to the Keystone controversy. Petroleum production in North America is now nearly 18 million barrels a day,[2] and could climb to 27 million barrels a day by 2020. Natural gas production in Canada and the United States could rise by a third over the same period, climbing to 22 billion cubic feet per day. This oil and gas will have to travel to where it is needed. Whether it is produced in Canada, Alaska, North Dakota, or the Gulf of Mexico, it will be used all over the country, especially since new environmental regulations are resulting in the rapid closures of coal-fired power plants, increasing the demand for natural gas as a substitute. Similarly, large fleets of buses and trucks are switching to natural gas, and General Motors and Chrysler are making dual-fuel pickup trucks.

This paper compares the record of transport via pipeline to that of road and rail and finds that pipelines are the safer option.

The first large-diameter long-distance pipelines were constructed during the Second World War, and they proliferated across the country over the ensuing two decades. Now America has 175,000 miles of onshore and offshore petroleum pipeline and 321,000 miles of natural gas transmission and gathering pipeline. In addition, over 2 million miles of natural gas distribution pipeline send natural gas to businesses and consumers.[3] This is expected to increase as households and businesses shift to natural gas to take advantage of low prices that are expected to last into the foreseeable future.

Pipelines are the primary mode of transportation for crude oil, petroleum products, and natural gas. Approximately 70 percent of crude oil and petroleum products are shipped by pipeline on a ton-mile basis. Tanker and barge traffic accounts for 23 percent of oil shipments. Trucking accounts for 4 percent of shipments, and rail for the remaining 3 percent. Essentially all dry natural gas is shipped by pipeline to end users.

If safety and environmental damages in the transportation of oil and gas were proportionate to the volume of shipments, one would expect the vast majority of damages to occur on pipelines. This paper finds the exact opposite. The majority of incidents occur on road and rail.

Data on pipeline safety are available from the United States Department of Transportation Pipeline and Hazardous Materials Safety Administration Office of Pipeline Safety (PHMSA).[4] Operators report to PHMSA any incident that crosses a certain safety threshold. These reports enable the public to compare the safety of pipelines to that of road and rail.

A pipeline incident must be reported if any of the following occur: (1) Explosion not intentionally set by the operator; (2)

Release of five gallons or more of a hazardous liquid (any petroleum or petroleum product) or carbon dioxide; (3) Fatality; (4) Personal injury necessitating hospitalization; and (5) Property damage, including cleanup costs, and the value of lost product, and the damage to the property of the operator or others, or both, estimated to exceed $50,000.[5]

One way to look at the safety record of petroleum, petroleum products, and natural gas pipeline operators is to examine PHMSA's aggregated data from individual reports. Property damage costs reported by PHMSA in 2011, with lost product accounted for at benchmark prices at the time of the incident.

To the untutored eye, it can appear that pipelines are prone to significant accidents. For instance, there were 721 incidents in 2005, and 53 fatalities in 1996, many caused by a propane explosion in San Juan. However, as the tables make clear, safety-related incidents, as measured by volume, are actually minor. More importantly, it is crucial to keep in mind that there is no way, in an advanced industrial economy, to avoid shipment of fuels to provide power. Crucially, by comparison with other means of such transport, pipelines emerge as relatively safe and reliable.

The number of incidents is relatively low. It has ranged from 339 in 1999 to 721 in 2005. Property damage has ranged from $53 million in 1995 to $1.3 billion in 2010. Lost barrels of liquids reached a low of 32,258 barrels in 2009 to a high of 123,419 the following year. Injuries ranged from 36 in 2006 to 127 in 1996, and fatalities ranged from 7 in 2001 to 53 in 1996.

The unusual increases in gross property damage in 2005 and 2010 were largely attributable to Hurricane Katrina in 2005 and the Kalamazoo River oil spill in 2010. Higher market prices for petroleum over the period has led to an increased valuation of spillage. Throughout the 1990s, apart from a brief price spike associated with the Persian Gulf War, the West Texas Intermediate wholesale price of oil stayed below $25 dollars per barrel. Prices continued to increase between 2000 and 2008, and averaged $100 in

2008. Prices eased in 2009 and 2010, but averaged around $95 in 2011 and $94 in 2012.[6]

A major criterion for determining if an incident had to be reported to PHMSA was significantly revised in 2002. Between 1992 and 2002 a spill only had to be reported if it was greater than 50 barrels of liquids or CO2 (after 1991). However, beginning in 2002, the limit was dropped to five gallons, with an exception for maintenance-related spills of five barrels or less confined to company sites.[7] Hence, minor spills that were not reported prior to 2002 were reported afterwards. From 1992 through 2001 an annual average of 383 incident reports were led with PHMSA. Then, from 2002 through 2011, companies led an annual average of 644 incident reports.

Gross barrels spilled do not take into account the number of barrels that were recovered during cleanup. The volume of liquids spilled that is ultimately recovered varies widely from year to year, and is likely heavily influenced by the nature of the spill. Between 1992 and 2011 about 40 percent of spilled liquids were recovered. Over the entire 20-year period a total of less than 1.5 million net barrels were spilled.

Volumes that are spilled are miniscule when compared to the volumes of petroleum that are used in the United States. To provide some prospective, U.S. refineries produce over 7 million barrels of gasoline every single day.[8] Considering the vast network, 175,000 miles of petroleum pipeline and over 2 million miles of natural gas pipelines (about 321,000 of transmission and gathering lines, over 2 million of local distribution main and service lines), incidents are exceedingly rare.[9]

To draw another comparison, according to the National Weather Service there was an average of 35 reported deaths annually caused by lightning from 2003 to 2012.[10] From 1992 to 2011 fatalities related to pipeline incidents were about 20 per year. An individual had a 75 percent greater chance of getting killed by lightning as being killed in a pipeline incident.

Data are also provided by PHMSA that make it possible to determine in what type of pipeline system a particular incident occurred. There are four basic categories of pipeline systems, namely hazardous liquids, natural gas gathering, natural gas transmission, and natural gas distribution. Natural gas gathering pipelines bring raw natural gas from the wellhead to the gas processing plant. The natural gas transmission system is made up of pipelines that bring processed (dry) gas from the plants and carry it across the country to city gates or to large customers (e.g., heavy industry or electrical power plants). The natural gas distribution system is operated by local distribution companies which transport gas from the city gate to local households and local businesses.

Although fatalities and injuries are relatively low, the majority of those that do occur have been associated with pipelines that are part of a natural gas distribution system. The U.S. natural gas distribution pipeline network spans over 2 million miles, and the federal government does not regulate intrastate pipelines (local distribution and production gathering lines), except for gathering lines that are located on federal lands. Local distribution companies, where both the vast majority of pipeline miles exist and accidents occur, are regulated by states and municipalities.

The proportion of property damage from incidents originating at hazardous liquids pipelines is largely the result of the inclusion of lost product as part of the damage, and that cleanup of oil spills is costly. From an operational standpoint, incidents associated with natural gas transmission and hazardous liquid systems (large diameter interstate pipelines) have resulted in 86 deaths and 387 injuries from 1992 through 2011.

How does this compare with road and rail? We have analyzed U.S. Department of Transportation data and produced incident and injury rates for oil and gas pipelines, road, and rail for petroleum products in the period 2005 through 2009.[11] Because reporting of pipeline incidents is only required for events involving injury or release over 5 gallons, we eliminated road and rail incidents not meeting those criteria from consideration. Even after this narrowing of scope, road and rail have higher rates of serious incidents and injuries than pipelines, even though more road and rail incidents go unreported.

Road had the highest rate of incidents, with 19.95 per billion ton miles per year. This was followed by rail, with 2.08 per billion ton miles per year. Natural gas transmission came next, with 0.89 per billion ton miles. Hazardous liquid pipelines were the safest, with 0.58 serious incidents per billion ton miles.

With respect to pipeline systems, natural gas transmission lines had the lowest average fatality rate for operator personnel and the general public between 2005 and 2009, with a rate of one person killed per year. This was followed by oil and rail, each with an average of 2.4 people per year. The rail figure is skewed by a chlorine incident on January 6, 2005 in Graniteville, South Carolina. The highest fatality rate is road, with an average of 10.2 people a year. This is not because members of the public are killed due to road accidents with oil trucks. Only 1.4 members of the public, on average, were killed annually, but an average of 8.8 operators died per year.

Rates of injury requiring hospitalization and of injury in general show a similar pattern. On average, annual injuries for 2005 through 2009 were lowest for hazardous liquid pipeline, at 4 people with injuries requiring hospitalization per year. The rate was higher for rail, at 4.6 of such injuries per year, although for rail this number was heavily biased by the 2005 observation. Road accidents hospitalized 8.8 people per year, and natural gas pipelines hospitalized 45 people each year.

The rates of injury per ton-mile are most pertinent, however. On this measure, hazardous liquid pipelines outperformed rail and road by a wide margin, causing just .0068 injuries requiring hospitalization per billion ton-miles. Rail caused nearly 30 times that many injuries requiring hospitalization on a per-ton- mile basis. Rail was also outperformed by natural gas pipelines on this measure, causing over 1.4 times as many serious injuries per ton- mile. Road was the worst performer on this measure, averaging one quarter serious injuries per billion ton-miles. This is 37 times the hazardous liquid pipeline rate.

Some claim that pipelines carrying Canadian oil sands crude, known as diluted bitumen, have more internal corrosion, and are subject to more incidents.[12] However, PHMSA data show that oil releases from corrosion are no more common in pipelines carrying Canadian diluted bitumen than in other lines.[13] Oil sands crude has been transported in American pipelines for the past decade.

The evidence is clear: transporting oil and natural gas by pipeline is safe. Furthermore, pipeline transportation is safer than transportation by road, rail, or barge, as measured by incidents, injuries, and fatalities—even though more road and rail incidents go unreported.[14]

Despite their safety, pipelines release more oil per spill than rail—but less than road. Typical release volumes on rail, particularly of petroleum products, are relatively low at 3,504 gallons per billion ton-miles. While it outperforms road in terms of product release per ton-mile, pipeline transport of petroleum products still experienced product release of 11,286 gallons per billion ton-miles. This figure does decrease by approximately one third if the high product-recovery rate for pipelines is considered, however. Volume release data are unavailable in the PHMSA incident database for natural gas transmission pipelines.

Rising oil and natural gas production is outpacing the transportation capacity of our inadequate national pipeline infrastructure. The Association of American Railroads reports that between 2008 and 2011 the total share of oil and gas rail shipments grew dramatically, from 2 percent of all carloads to 11 percent.[15] In 2011 alone, rail capacity in the Bakken area—stretching from southern Alberta to the northern U.S. Great Plains—tripled to almost 300,000 barrels per day.[16] Crude oil shipments via rail have continued to expand at an accelerating rate; as of September 2012, U.S. Class I railroads were on pace to deliver 200,000 carloads of crude for the year, compared to just 66,000 in 2011 and 9,500 in 2008.[17]

As America continues to ramp up production of oil and natural gas, our pipeline infrastructure becomes more important. We need better pipelines to get oil from North Dakota to the refineries in the Gulf, and natural gas from the Marcellus Shale in Pennsylvania (and New York, should the Empire State allow production to move forward) and the Utica Shale in Ohio to the rest of the country. In the next few years, the Obama administration may allow more states to explore for oil offshore. In addition, Congress might vote to give coastal areas a share of oil drilling revenue, providing a powerful incentive for more drilling. Congress could also form a liability risk pool to allow independent drillers to expand into the Gulf of Mexico. In order for these resources to get where they are needed, America needs more pipelines—the safest way to move fuel.

Endnotes

1. Reliable data on water-borne spills, which fall under the jurisdiction of the Coast Guard, are not readily available and so will not be included in this Issue Brief

2. International Energy Statistics, "Petroleum Production," accessed May 7, 2013, http://www.eia.gov/cfapps/ipdbproject/iedindex3.cfm?tid=5&pid=53&aid=1

3. "Pipeline Basics," The United States Department of Transportation Pipeline and Hazardous Materials Safety Administration Office of Pipeline Safety, accessed May 7, 2013, http://primis.phmsa.dot.gov/comm/PipelineBasics.htm?nocache=8264

4. "Community Toolbox," The United States Department of Transportation Pipeline and Hazardous Materials Safety Administration Office of Pipeline Safety, accessed April 24, 2012, http://primis.phmsa.dot.gov/comm/Index.htm?nocache=4323

5. "Reporting Criteria Changes," The United States Department of Transportation Pipeline and Hazardous Materials Safety Administration Office of Pipeline Safety, accessed April 24, 2012, http://primis.phmsa.dot.gov/comm/reports/safety/docs/IncidentReportingCriteriaHistory1990-2011.pdf

6. "Petroleum and Other Liquids, Spot Prices," United States Energy Information Agency, accessed May 7, 2013, http://www.eia.gov/dnav/pet/pet_pri_spt_s1_a.htm

7. "Reporting Criteria Changes 1990-Current," The United States Department of Transportation Pipeline and Hazardous Materials Safety Administration Office of Pipeline Safety, last updated March 2011, http://primis.phmsa.dot.gov/comm/reports/safety/docs/IncidentReportingCriteriaHistory1990-2011.pdf

8. U.S. Energy Information Agency, *This Week In Petroleum*, accessed May 20, 2013, http://www.eia.gov/oog/info/twip/twip_crude.html#production

9. "Pipeline Basics," The United States Department of Transportation Pipeline and Hazardous Materials Safety Administration Office of Pipeline Safety, accessed April 24, 2012, http://primis.phmsa.dot.gov/comm/PipelineBasics.htm?nocache=8264

10. National Weather Service, "Weather Fatalities," 2012, http://www.nws.noaa.gov/om/hazstats.shtml

11. U.S. Department of Transportation, Pipeline and Hazardous Materials Safety Administration, Office of Pipeline Safety, *Building Safe Communities: Pipeline Risk and its Application to Local Development Decisions*, October, 2010, http://www.pstrust.org/library/docs/PIPA-PipelineRiskReport-Final-20101021.pdf

12. See, for example, Lara Skinner and Sean Sweeney, "The Impact of Tar Sands Pipeline Spills on Employment and the Economy," Cornell University Global Labor Institute, March, 2012

13. U.S. Department of Transportation, Pipeline and Hazardous Materials Safety Administration, data from form PHMSA F 7000-1

14. Committee on Transportation and Infrastructure hearings on "Concerns with Hazardous Materials Safety in the U.S.: Is PHMSA Performing Its Mission?" (written report submitted by Majority Staff to the Members of the Committee), September 9, 2009

15. "EIA: Rail Delivery of Crude Oil and Petroleum Products Rising," Crude Oil Trader, accessed June 05, 2012, http://crudeoiltrader.blogspot.com/2011/11/eia-rail-delivery-of-crude-oil-and.html

16. "Buffet's Burlington Northern Among Pipeline Winners," Bloomberg News, accessed June 05, 2012, http://www.bloomberg.com/news/2012-01-23/buffett-s-burlington-northern-among-winners-in-obama-rejection-of-pipeline. html

17. Association of American Railroads, "Moving Crude Petroleum by Rail," December 2012, https://www.aar.org/keyissues/Documents/Background-Papers/Moving%20Crude%20Petroleum%20by%20Rail%202012-12-10.pdf

8

Pipeline Spills Create Economic Opportunity—but at What Cost?

David Suzuki

David Suzuki is the co-founder of the David Suzuki Foundation and a Professor Emeritus at the University of British Columbia. As an award-winning scientist, environmentalist and writer, he has created and hosted numerous television and radio specials that explain natural science in an entertaining and easy to understand way.

Oil spills provide economic opportunities. They're terrible for the environment but are unfortunately good for business by creating jobs, and providing tax payments to governments. But what is at stake? David Suzuki breaks it all down in the following viewpoint, noting that people must learn to live with less, and governments and businesses must help wean the population off of fossil fuels so the planet will not be destroyed.

Energy giant Kinder Morgan was recently called insensitive for pointing out that "Pipeline spills can have both positive and negative effects on local and regional economies, both in the short- and long-term." The company wants to triple its shipping capacity from the Alberta tar sands to Burnaby, in part by twinning its current pipeline. Its National Energy Board submission states, "Spill response and cleanup creates business and employment

"Yes, Pipeline Spills Are Good For The Economy," by David Suzuki, The David Suzuki Foundation, June 12, 2014. Reprinted by Permission.

opportunities for affected communities, regions, and cleanup service providers."

It may seem insensitive, but it's true. And that's the problem. Destroying the environment is bad for the planet and all the life it supports, including us. But it's often good for business. The 2010 BP oil spill in the Gulf of Mexico added billions to the U.S. gross domestic product! Even if a spill never occurred (a big "if," considering the records of Kinder Morgan and other pipeline companies), increasing capacity from 300,000 to 890,000 barrels a day would go hand-in-hand with rapid tar sands expansion and more wasteful, destructive burning of fossil fuels—as would approval of Enbridge Northern Gateway and other pipeline projects, as well as increased oil shipments by rail.

The company will make money, the government will reap some tax and royalty benefits and a relatively small number of jobs will be created. But the massive costs of dealing with a pipeline or tanker spill and the resulting climate change consequences will far outweigh the benefits. Of course, under our current economic paradigm, even the costs of responding to global warming impacts show as positive growth in the GDP—the tool we use to measure what passes for progress in this strange worldview.

And so it's full speed ahead and damn the consequences. Everything is measured in money. B.C.'s economy seems sluggish? Well, obviously, the solution is to get fracking and sell the gas to Asian markets. Never mind that a recent study, commissioned by the Canadian government, concludes we don't know enough about the practice to say it's safe, the federal government has virtually no regulations surrounding it and provincial rules "are not based on strong science and remain untested." Never mind that the more infrastructure we build for polluting, climate-disrupting fossil fuels, the longer it will take us to move away from them. There's easy money to be had—for someone.

We need to do more than just get off fossil fuels, although that's a priority. We need to conserve, cut back and switch to cleaner energy sources. In Canada, we need a national energy strategy.

And guess what? That will create lasting jobs! But we must also find better ways to run our societies than relying on rampant consumption, planned obsolescence, excessive and often-pointless work and an economic system that depends on damaging ways and an absurd measurement to convince us it somehow all amounts to progress.

It's not about going back to the Dark Ages. It's about realizing that a good life doesn't depend on owning more stuff, scoring the latest gadgets or driving bigger, faster cars. Our connections with family, friends, community and nature are vastly more important.

Yes, we need oil and gas, and will for some time. Having built our cities and infrastructure to accommodate cars rather than people, we can't turn around overnight. But we can stop wasting our precious resources. By conserving and switching to cleaner energy, we can ensure we still have oil and gas long into the future, perhaps long enough to learn to appreciate the potential of what's essentially energy from the sun, stored and compressed over millions of years. If we dig it up and sell it so it can be burned around the world, we consign ourselves to a polluted planet ravaged by global warming, with nothing to fall back on when fossil fuels are gone.

Scientists around the world have been warning us for decades about the consequences of our wasteful lifestyles, and evidence for the ever-increasing damage caused by pollution and climate change continues to grow. But we have to do more than just wean ourselves off fossil fuels. We must also look to economic systems, progress measurements and ways of living that don't depend on destroying everything the planet provides to keep us healthy and alive.

9

Aging Pipelines Are Accidents Waiting to Happen

Elizabeth Shogren

Elizabeth Shogren is a correspondent for High Country News *and is based in Washington, D.C. Shogren also served as environmental correspondent for National Public Radio for more than a decade.*

An oil spill near Little Rock, Arkansas, demonstrates what many fear—aging energy pipelines are catastrophes waiting to happen, and in this case a resident reported seeing "a river" of oil out her front door. Environmental reporter Elizabeth Shogren relates the shocking—and edifying—details in the following viewpoint. Worthy of note: The head of the National Transportation Safety Board claims that of the twenty accidents investigated by her agency, all of them could have been prevented.

Amber Bartlett was waiting last Friday for her kids to come home from school. One of them called from the entrance to the upscale subdivision near Little Rock, Ark., to tell her the community was being evacuated because of an oil spill. Bartlett was amazed by what she saw out her front door.

"I mean, just rolling oil. I mean, it was like a river," she says. "It had little waves in it."

"Arkansas Oil Spill Sheds Light On Aging Pipeline System," by Elizabeth Shogren, NPR, April 4, 2013. Reprinted by Permission.

ExxonMobil, the company that runs the pipeline, says it has collected hundreds of thousands of gallons of oil and water from Bartlett's neighborhood.

Bartlett says things could have been much worse. Her children's baby-sitter lives in the house closest to where the pipeline burst.

"They play right there every day where it busted," she says. "We are fortunate our babies were not out there during that time."

Bartlett says ExxonMobil has paid hotel bills, fed families and even given children Easter baskets.

"I'm upset," she says. "But accidents happen."

"It Is Catastrophic"

It's not yet clear what caused the spill. Exxon's Pegasus pipeline is 65 years old. It runs 858 miles from Illinois to Texas. It was adapted a few years ago to increase its capacity by 50 percent.

Arkansas Attorney General Dustin McDaniel, who is investigating the spill, visited the subdivision Wednesday.

"I have been reminded by Exxon's representatives that this is a relatively small spill and cleanup is going just great," he said. "I hope that they realize that to the homeowners in this area, it is not small—it is catastrophic."

McDaniel said he knows underground pipelines are essential to keeping the country's economy going. They carry fuel for cars, airplanes and home furnaces.

"We got to have that, but it has to be maintained," he said. "It has to be inspected."

McDaniel said Exxon has repeatedly told him that inspections were up to date and showed no cause for concern. He said the spill raises questions about whether the inspection process for aging pipelines is adequate.

In fact, more than half of the nation's pipelines were built before 1970. More than 2.5 million miles of pipelines run underground throughout the country. According to federal statistics, they have on average 280 significant spills a year. Most of these accidents aren't big enough to make headlines.

Accidents Preventable?

The National Transportation Safety Board has investigated 20 pipeline accidents since 2000. Debbie Hersman, who heads the agency, says by and large the system is safe.

"But that still doesn't mean that we should accept these accidents when they occur," she says. "Particularly if you can demonstrate that they are preventable. And I will tell you, 100 percent of the accidents that we've investigated were completely preventable."

Hersman says her investigators repeatedly find the same problems—for example, cracks and corrosion that were discovered by inspections but never fixed.

"If companies invest in safety, we can get to zero accidents in the pipeline industry," she says.

John Stoody, director for government and public relations at the Association of Oil Pipe Lines, stresses that pipelines' safety record is getting better.

"We spend over a billion dollars every year inspecting the pipelines, checking them for any issues, performing maintenance on them as they're needed," he says. "And it's something we care a lot about. We certainly want to have as few incidents as possible."

Stoody says pipelines are the safest way to transport the fuel people need for their daily lives. He notes that 99.995 percent of petroleum barrels reach their destination safely.

But Anthony Swift, an attorney for the environmental group Natural Resources Defense Counsel, says that's "not a particularly comforting statistic if you look at the sheer amount of crude oil spilled."

Federal data show that on average over the past decade, nearly 3.5 million gallons of oil spilled from pipelines each year.

Swift says the spill in Arkansas sends a wake-up call: It's a reminder of the real risks of an aging pipeline system.

10

Explaining the Protests Over the Dakota Access Pipeline

Brad Plumer

Brad Plumer directs the coverage of science, environment, and energy topics as a senior editor at Vox.com. Previously, Plumer reported on issues about climate and energy policy for The Washington Post.

Various Native American tribes, environmental supporters, authorities, and others have joined the Standing Rock Sioux Tribe to battle against implementation of the Dakota Access Pipeline, and senior editor Brad Plumer explains the brass tacks of the conflict in the following viewpoint. Ever since the proposal in 2014, the pipeline has been controversial. After being three-fourths completed, then President Obama halted the project, but the energy company behind the pipeline expects Donald Trump to go ahead with the project.

For months, the Standing Rock Sioux Tribe in North Dakota has been waging a pitched battle against a proposed oil pipeline that would run near their reservation—arguing that it would endanger both their water supplies and sacred sites.

These protests have become a huge, huge story. The fight over the Dakota Access Pipeline encompasses everything from the federal government's historically appalling treatment of Native Americans to broader debates about fracking and climate change. The cause has attracted an array of tribes, activists, and

"The Battle Over the Dakota Access Pipeline, Explained," by Brad Plumer, Vox Media, Inc, November 29, 2016. Reprinted by Permission.

environmentalists around the country, and authorities have been clashing with protestors all summer.

On Sunday, these clashes turned violent when law-enforcement officials used water cannons on protesters in freezing weather—sending some 26 people to the hospital with bone fractures or hypothermia. This came after an earlier major confrontation on October 27, when activists occupied private land along the pipeline's proposed route, arguing that it actually belonged to the tribes under an 1851 treaty with the US government that hasn't been properly honored. In response, police used rubber bullets, pepper spray, and water cannons to disperse the protestors, arresting 141 people in all.

Opponents have also taken the fight to court, hoping to alter or block the pipeline. The DC Circuit Court is currently hearing a major legal challenge to the project, with the Standing Rock Sioux arguing that the Army Corps of Engineers did not properly consult them before green-lighting the section near their reservation.

The pipeline is now 75 percent complete, but it's hit some serious roadblocks. On September 9, the Obama administration ordered the Army Corps of Engineers to pause further permitting and revisit the controversial section nearest the reservation. Then, on November 2, President Obama said that officials are looking into possible ways to reroute the project, though a decision could take weeks. The pipeline company, for its part, is hoping Donald Trump will approve the project when he comes to office.

All the while, protests continue to grow. So here's a guide to how we got this point.

What is the Dakota Access Pipeline?

The pipeline in question was first proposed in 2014 by Dakota Access, a subsidiary of Texas-based Energy Transfer Partners. If built, it would carry some 450,000 barrels of crude per day from the Bakken oil fields in North Dakota down to a terminal in Illinois, where it could be shipped to refineries and turned into usable fuel.

The whole thing would stretch 1,134 miles underground and cost some $3.8 billion.

The rationale behind this project is straightforward. Since the late 2000s, drillers have been using fracking techniques to exploit vast new deposits of oil in the shale formations of North Dakota. Crude oil output has surged, and the state has become one of the epicenters of the recent US oil boom.

But because this all happened so quickly, there weren't sufficient pipelines to carry all that new oil to market. Instead, North Dakota's drillers have been shipping thousands of barrels of crude each day by trains, which are costlier and also sometimes get derailed and explode. Oil companies would prefer a cheaper, quieter pipeline, especially now that crude prices have dropped and profits are thinner. Hence the proposal.

Why is the Dakota Access Pipeline So Controversial?

Although oil pipelines are less accident-prone than trains, they've certainly been known to leak, with destructive results. So there's been scattered complaints about the proposed route ever since late 2014, starting with farmers in Iowa.

But by far the biggest source of opposition has been in North Dakota, around the portion of pipeline that would run just north of Sioux County and the Standing Rock Indian Reservation, home to 8,250 people.

For months, members of the Standing Rock Sioux have raised two major concerns about the project:

- First, the pipeline would cross right under the Missouri River at Lake Oahe, half a mile north of the reservation. A leak or spill could send oil directly into the tribe's main source of drinking water. The tribe points out that Dakota Access originally considered a route farther north, upstream of Bismarck, but the company rejected that route, in part, because of the close proximity to the state capital's drinking-water wells.

- Second, the tribe argues that the pipeline would run through a stretch of land north of the reservation that contains recently discovered sacred sites and burial places. True, this land isn't part of the current reservation. But the Standing Rock Sioux argue that the land had been taken away from them unjustly over the past 150 years. And any bulldozing and construction work could damage these sites.

As such, the tribe has called on the pipeline to be rerouted or reconsidered altogether. (In response, Dakota Access has argued that it will employ "new advanced pipeline technology" to limit leaks—and that it will take care to protect any cultural sites.)

More to the point, the Standing Rock Sioux argue that under federal law, the US government should have consulted extensively with the tribe about these issues—and didn't. On July 27, the Standing Rock Sioux and the nonprofit Earthjustice sued the Army Corps of Engineers in federal court, arguing that the agency had wrongly approved the pipeline without adequate consultation.

As journalist Aura Bogado explains, at the core of this dispute is the concept of "tribal sovereignty." The US government is supposed to have a "government-to-government" relationship with native tribes—not run roughshod over them.

What are the Dakota Access Pipeline Protests?

Since March, thousands of Native Americans from across the country have come to Cannon Ball to camp out and protest the pipeline in solidarity with the Standing Rock Sioux.

The fight has attracted the interest of climate activists and environmentalists, who have been focused on blocking new fossil fuel infrastructure, particularly after their victory in stopping the Keystone XL pipeline last year. It's also pulled in politicians like Bernie Sanders and Jill Stein. (Hillary Clinton, by contrast, has avoided taking a stand.)

The last few months in particular have seen the battle intensify. This new phase began around August 24, after the Standing Rock

Sioux asked the DC Circuit Court for an injunction to halt activity on the pipeline while their broader lawsuit against the project was resolved (a lawsuit that could take a year or more).

Then, on September 3, shortly after the injunction was requested, Dakota Access deployed bulldozers and began digging up the section of the pipeline route that contained possible native burial artifacts—widely viewed as an attempt to circumvent the lawsuit and make the pipeline inevitable. Protesters tried to stop the bulldozers, and there's video of private security responding with dogs and pepper spray.

Five days later, North Dakota Gov. Jack Dalrymple activated the state National Guard "in the event they are needed to support law enforcement response efforts."

In October, protestors began occupying a portion of privately owned land just north of the reservation that lay directly in the pipeline's path. They've argued that this slice of land actually belongs to Native Americans under the Fort Laramie Treaty of 1851, signed between eight tribes and the US government—a treaty that was subsequently violated after Congress unilaterally took back territory over the years. "We have never ceded this land," said Joye Braun of the Indigenous Environmental Network in a statement.

The protestors on the private land say their demonstrations have been peaceful, featuring prayers and chants and drum circles. But local authorities have cracked down hard on these intrusions: On October 27, police used pepper spray, water cannons, and bean bags to push back the activists, arresting more than 141 people in all.

On November 21, the clashes took another violent turn as law enforcement officials used water cannons in subzero temperatures to beat back a crowd of 400 people. (The Morton County sheriff's office claimed that protestors had been setting fires.) According to the *Guardian*, at least 26 people were hospitalized—some with bone fractures, most with hypothermia.

What's the Lawsuit Over the Pipeline All About?

While the protests rage on, there's also a court case winding through federal courts that could decide the ultimate fate of the pipeline. The case centers around the Army Corps of Engineers, the federal agency that typically approves interstate pipelines and provides permit for water crossings.

By law, any federal agency overseeing a construction project has to consult with native nations or tribes if there are places with "religious and cultural significance" nearby. (This is true even if those places are not explicitly part of a reservation—a recognition that many tribes have been forcibly relocated by the federal government and have had their lands taken over the years.)

In their complaint, filed on July 27, the Standing Rock Sioux argued that the Army Corps of Engineers handed out water permits too hastily and only consulted with the tribe on a narrow set of potential impacts. (The tribe ended up sitting out much of the consultation process in protest.) The tribe also argued that Dakota Access used out-of-state experts to survey the lands beforehand, and so missed a whole bunch of culturally significant archaeological discoveries along the pipeline's path.

You should read Robinson Meyer in the *Atlantic* for much more on the legal merits of the case. He argues that the Standing Rock Sioux have a reasonable case—the law is pretty clear that native nations or tribes need to be consulted extensively, in a "government-to-government" fashion. But it's far from clear they'll actually win.

This case is currently being heard by US District Judge James E. Boasberg, who was appointed to the federal bench by President Obama in 2011. It could take months to reach a resolution. So, in the meantime, the Standing Rock Sioux and the nonprofit Earthjustice had asked for an injunction to halt construction until a final decision.

On September 9, Boasberg denied that request for an injunction. He starts by setting the scene: "Since the founding of this nation, the United States' relationship with the Indian tribes has been contentious and tragic." But he then goes on to argue that the tribe "has not shown it will suffer injury that would be prevented by any injunction the Court could issue" and that the Army Corps "gave the Tribe a reasonable and good-faith opportunity to identify sites of importance to it."

Immediately after the injunction was denied, however, the Obama administration stepped in and ordered a stop to construction around Lake Oahe until the Army Corps of Engineers could revisit the disputes over this portion of the pipeline. "Furthermore," the Department of Justice, Department of Interior, and Department of the Army said in a letter, "this case has highlighted the need for a serious discussion on whether there should be nationwide reform with respect to considering tribes' views on these types of infrastructure projects."

What Happens Next for the Pipeline?

On November 2, as protests continued, Obama issued another statement saying that the Army Corps "is examining whether there are ways to reroute this pipeline." He added: "[W]e're going to let it play out for several more weeks and determine whether or not this can be resolved in a way that I think is properly attentive to the traditions of the first Americans." (There's a piece from E&E on whether rerouting the project is even possible—certainly it would cost developers millions of dollars.)

For now, the portion of the pipeline nearest the reservation remains in limbo and the legal battles will continue. As Earthjustice explains, the broader lawsuit against the pipeline is still moving forward—and may not get resolved before the end of 2016, at least. What's more, Dakota Access still must get one last bit of approval from the Army Corps of Engineers before digging on either side of Lake Oahe. On November 14, the Army Corps called for "additional discussion" with the Sioux before deciding to grant that final permit.

Looming over all of this, of course, is the specter of Donald Trump. The company behind the project, Energy Transfer Partners, has said that it fully expects Trump's administration to approve the pipeline come January. The company's CEO, Kelcy Warren, donated $100,000 to a Trump Victory Fund before the election. (Trump himself reportedly once held stock in Energy Transfer Partners worth over $500,000, though a spokesperson told the *Washington Post* he sold it off earlier this summer.)

Still, nothing's settled yet. And, in the meantime, protestors aren't backing down. Here's Dave Archambault II, chairman of the Standing Rock Sioux, in September: "We're going to continue to [fight this battle] as long as it takes to try and have this nation recognize the injustices that are being implemented on our nation."

11

Destructive Effects Linger After Oil Spill

Debbie Elliott

Debbie Elliott is a National Public Radio National Correspondent who covers issues important to the South, where she grew up.

After the Deepwater Horizon Oil rig exploded in the Gulf of Mexico disastrous effects took hold of the area immediately. NPR correspondent Debbie Elliott offers key insights about the incident in the following viewpoint—revealing that from Texas to Florida, people, wildlife, and the environment suffered as a result. British Petroleum (BP), and some city officials report that conditions have improved, but a Louisiana outdoorsman and a Alabama oysterman contend otherwise.

Five years ago, BP's out-of-control oil well deep in the Gulf of Mexico exploded. Eleven workers were killed on the Deepwater Horizon rig. But it was more than a deadly accident—the blast unleashed the nation's worst offshore environmental catastrophe.

In the spring and summer of 2010, oil gushed from the Macondo well for nearly three months. More than 3 million barrels of Louisiana light crude fouled beaches and wetlands from Texas to Florida, affecting wildlife and livelihoods.

Today, the spill's impacts linger.

"5 Years After BP Oil Spill, Effects Linger And Recovery Is Slow," by Debbie Elliott, NPR, April 20, 2015. Reprinted by Permission.

Buried Oil, Brought Back By The Surf

On a remote string of barrier islands off the Louisiana coast, longtime outdoorsman Bob Marshall, an environmental writer for *The Lens*, steers his Twin Vee catamaran toward East Grand Terre. Marshall was on this island when the oil hit the shore in 2010.

"I'll never forget the day it came in here," he says. "It was the peak nesting season in April for brown pelicans."

He describes waves of reddish-orange gunk rolling in with the tide.

"It was hitting these islands, coating the roots of the mangroves and also the birds were diving," Marshall says. "The adults would come back after looking for food and sit down on their eggs and there was oil on the eggs."

This was one of the most heavily oiled areas during the BP oil spill five years ago. Today, hundreds of tar balls still dot the beach. A BP crew works to clean up a large tar mat from the surf.

"This will be going on, unfortunately, for years," says Marshall.

That's because some of the oil was buried beneath the sand just offshore, and it gets churned up when the surf is rough. Back out on Barataria Bay, Marshall points to where roots jut up in the open water. These used to be mangrove islands.

"The oil coated the roots of those mangrove trees and then they died," Marshall says. "And without the mangroves to hold the islands together, within three years most of those islands were gone."

Louisiana was already losing land at an alarming rate, but scientists confirm that the oil spill accelerated the pace. Barataria Bay has lost key bird nesting islands, and federal government studies indicate that dolphins here in the bay are sick and dying at a higher rate than normal and show signs of oil poisoning.

On an afternoon boat tour, Marshall sees something that worries him.

"There's another dead dolphin. That's the second one we've seen," he notes. "This is strictly anecdotal—can't tie it to anything.

But seriously, I've never seen a single dead dolphin out here. Now I'm seeing two. This is amazing."

BP: "The Gulf Is A Resilient Body Of Water"

Cynthia Sarthou, executive director of Gulf Restoration Network, says that after five years, there are more questions than answers about what the lingering impact of the spill means.

"Dolphin deaths continue, oil is still on the bottom of the ocean, tar balls keep coming up," she says. "And nobody really is able to say what we may find in five years, 10 years. It's really distressing to me."

Sarthou says there's no certainty the spill won't be a problem for generations to come.

"It's not publicly seen but it is out there. It's in the marine environment," she says. "And so whether we see it or not the potential impacts of its presence may plague us for decades."

But BP senior vice president Geoff Morrell says the signs are good for a healthy Gulf.

"There is nothing to suggest other than that the Gulf is a resilient body of water that has bounced back strongly," he says. "The Gulf has not been damaged anywhere near the degree some people feared it would have in the midst of the spill."

Under federal law, BP will have to pay to restore the damage to natural resources caused by its spill—a scientific assessment that is ongoing and could take years to resolve.

BP also faces a court judgment that could top $13 billion in an ongoing liability case. A New Orleans federal judge has ruled that BP's gross negligence and willful misconduct are to blame for the disaster.

Morrell says BP has already spent $28 billion on response and cleanup and to pay economic claims to oil spill victims. He says the company has changed its safety procedures, and pre-deployed capping stacks around the world that could more quickly shut down an out-of-control well.

"The Deepwater Horizon accident was a tragedy. It was deeply regrettable," says Morrell. "And we have done everything possible to learn from it."

There's no sign of oil on the breezy public beach in Gulf Shores, Ala., where kids play in the surf. The line of colorful umbrellas today along the pristine white sand is a far cry from five years ago.

"Five years ago you'd see oil all over our beach and you'd see no people here," says Mayor Robert Craft. "Our beaches were ruined."

Now Craft says they have recovered and visitors are coming back. But the disaster was a huge blow, both economically and environmentally, and he's not sure it's over.

"Economically we're doing really well and the environment seems to be short-term looking well, too," he says. "But what we don't know is the long-term environmental consequences of this. It just hasn't been long enough to know."

Some Industries Still Reeling

Tourists have flocked back to the beaches of Alabama, Mississippi and the Florida Panhandle, helped in part by an ad campaign paid for by BP.

Other coastal industries are still trying to come back.

In Bon Secour, Ala., fourth-generation oysterman Chris Nelson shows off his family's seafood processing plant, Bon Secour Fisheries. About a dozen shuckers are at work at stainless steel tables, slipping a knife into oyster shells to extract the meat.

"We call this our opening house," Nelson says. "A lot of people call this a shucking house."

Half the tables here are idle.

"Our business is still struggling here at Bon Secour Fisheries because of the lack of oyster production," Nelson says. "I place the blame for that on the oil spill."

Nelson is on the Gulf States Marine Fisheries Commission. He says one of the most productive public oyster reefs in the country—east of the Mississippi river off the Louisiana coast—is not producing like it should.

"That was maybe not coincidentally the closest place to where the spill was occurring, where the leak was," Nelson says. "That area still has not produced an appreciable number of oysters, and has not recruited any young oysters to speak of since the spill."

Nelson says it's not clear whether the reef was harmed by exposure to oil, or by the freshwater that was released in Louisiana in hopes of pushing it away. Either way, he says, it's a problem that needs resolving.

"The economy of this region has been damaged tremendously," Nelson says. "BP has done a lot to bring us back. But again the commitment by both the administration and by BP was to get us back better than we were before. I don't think we're better than we were before."

12

Raw, Corrosive Tar Sands Oil Is Cause for Concern

Anthony Swift, Susan Casey-Lefkowitz, and Elizabeth Shope

Anthony Swift, Susan Casey-Lefkowitz and Elizabeth Shope all work with the Natural Resources Defense Council (NRDC), which teams more than two million members and online activists with some 500 scientists, lawyers, and policy advocates across the globe to ensure the rights of all people to the air, the water, and the wild.

In the past, the United States has imported a form of synthetic crude oil from Canada. This has changed, and the new form of oil being shipped, DilBit, is quite worrisome because of its dangerous characteristics, which concerned NRDC members detail in the following report. The three authors encourage additional safety measures in order to protect the many water systems and animal habitats that the carrying pipelines may affect.

Tar Sands Movement into the United States

Tar sands crude oil pipeline companies are using conventional pipeline technology to transport diluted bitumen or "DilBit," a highly corrosive, acidic, and potentially unstable blend of thick raw bitumen and volatile natural gas liquid condensate. In order to become usable transportation fuels, DilBit can only be processed by certain refineries that have built the capacity to handle very

"Tar Sands Pipelines Safety Risks," by Anthony Swift, Susan Casey-Lefkowitz and Elizabeth Shope, Natural Resources Defense Council, February 2011. Included with permission from the Natural Resources Defense Council.

heavy crudes. With Canadian upgraders operating at full capacity, oil companies have started transporting more of the raw tar sands to U.S. refineries that can either already take the heavier oil or need to build additional upgrading capacity.

Historically, the United States has imported the majority of tar sands crude from Canada in the form of synthetic crude oil, a substance similar to conventional crude oil that has already gone through an initial upgrading process. Importing tar sands oil into the United States as DilBit—instead of synthetic crude oil—is a recent and growing development.[1] Without much public knowledge or a change in safety standards, U.S. pipelines are carrying increasing amounts of the corrosive raw form of tar sands oil. In fact, over the last ten years, DilBit exports to the United States have increased almost fivefold, to 550,000 barrels per day (bpd) in 2010—more than half of the approximately 900,000 bpd of tar sands oil currently flowing into the United States.[2] By 2019, Canadian tar sands producers plan to triple this amount to as much as 1.5 million bpd of DilBit.[3]

DilBit is the primary product being transported through the new TransCanada Keystone pipeline that runs from Alberta's tar sands to Illinois and Oklahoma,[4] and also through Enbridge's recently-built Alberta Clipper pipeline, which terminates in Wisconsin.[5] In addition, DilBit is transported through the existing Enbridge Lakehead system that brings both conventional oil and tar sands from the Canadian border to Minnesota, Wisconsin, Illinois, Indiana, and Michigan.

Transporting DilBit is also the primary purpose of TransCanada's proposed Keystone XL pipeline, which would run nearly 2000 miles from Alberta through some of America's most sensitive lands and aquifers on the way to refineries on the U.S. Gulf Coast.[6] This infrastructure will lock the United States into a continued reliance on pipelines that may not be operated or regulated adequately to meet the unique safety requirements for DilBit for decades to come.

DilBit Pipeline Safety Concerns

As tar sands oil companies send increasing volumes of DilBit to the United States, the risks of pipeline spills are becoming more apparent. DilBit pipelines, which require higher operating temperatures and pressures to move the thick material through a pipe, appear to pose new and significant risks of pipeline leaks or ruptures due to corrosion, as well as problems with leak detection and safety problems from the instability of DilBit. For example, in July 2010, an Enbridge tar sands pipeline spilled over 840,000 gallons of diluted bitumen into Michigan's Kalamazoo River watershed.

[...]

DilBit is Risky to the Environment and Human Health

DilBit poses an elevated risk to the environment and public safety once a leak has occurred. While all crude oil spills are potentially hazardous, the low flash point and high vapor pressure of the natural gas liquid condensate used to dilute the DilBit increase the risk of the leaked material exploding.[7] DilBit can form an ignitable and explosive mixture in the air at temperatures above 0 degrees Fahrenheit.[8] This mixture can be ignited by heat, spark, static charge, or flame.[9] In addition, one of the potential toxic products of a DilBit explosion is hydrogen sulfide, a gas which can cause suffocation in concentrations over 100 parts per million and is identified by producers as a potential hazard associated with a DilBit spill.[9] Enbridge identified hydrogen sulfide as a potential risk to its field personnel during its cleanup of the Kalamazoo River spill.[10]

DilBit contains benzene, polycyclic aromatic hydrocarbons, and n-hexane, toxins that can affect the human central nervous systems.[11] A recent report filed by the Michigan Department of Community Health found that nearly 60 percent of individuals living in the vicinity of the Kalamazoo River spill experienced respiratory, gastrointestinal, and neurological symptoms consistent with acute exposure to benzene and other petroleum related chemicals.[12] In addition to their short term effects, long term exposure to benzene and polycyclic aromatic hydrocarbons has been known to cause cancer.[13]

DilBit also contains vanadium, nickel, arsenic, and other heavy metals in significantly larger quantities than occur in conventional crude.[14] These heavy metals have a variety of toxic effects, are not biodegradable, and can accumulate in the environment to become health hazards to wildlife and people.[15]

[…]

DilBit Putting U.S. Special Places at Risk [16]

With more DilBit coming into the United States in pipelines built under conventional oil standards, it is important to understand the water resources, habitat, and wildlife at risk from existing DilBit pipelines throughout the Midwest as well as from the proposed Keystone XL pipeline to Texas.

Great Lakes

The Great Lakes are the largest source of freshwater in the world, and provide drinking water for 40 million American and Canadian citizens.[17] Enbridge pipelines that sometimes carry DilBit run through the Great Lakes region close to Lake Superior, Lake Michigan, Lake Huron, and Lake Erie.[18]

Lake St. Clair and the St. Clair River

The St. Clair River provides drinking water for millions in Southeast Michigan and was threatened by a potentially faulty section of the Enbridge pipeline that runs under the river and is due to be replaced in early 2011.[19] The St. Clair River drains into Lake St. Clair, the Detroit River, and Lake Erie.

Indiana Dunes

Enbridge pipelines run near the biologically rich and recreationally important Indiana Dunes, on the southern shore of Lake Michigan.[20]

Deep Fork Wildlife Management Area

In Oklahoma, the proposed Keystone XL pipeline would cut through this 11,900 acre haven for game and non-game species, including Bobwhite Quail, turkeys, bobcats, and Bald Eagles.[21]

Native Prairies and the Threatened Topeka Shiner Minnow

In Kansas, the proposed Keystone XL pipeline would cross native prairies and may affect critically designated habitat for the federally endangered Topeka Shiner minnow.[22]

Whooping Crane and Sandhill Crane Habitat

The proposed Keystone XL pipeline would cross the Platte River in Nebraska, an important stopover site on the migration path of the endangered Whooping Crane. Sandhill Cranes also use the area as a nesting site.[23]

Ogallala Aquifer

The proposed Keystone XL pipeline crosses the Ogallala Aquifer, one of the world's largest freshwater aquifers that provides 30 percent of the ground water used for irrigation in the United States, and drinking water for millions of Americans. The aquifer covers areas in South Dakota, Nebraska, Wyoming, Colorado, Kansas, Oklahoma, New Mexico, and Texas.

Prairie Potholes and Migratory Birds

In South Dakota, the Keystone XL pipeline route tracks the Central and Mississippi migratory bird flyways, and cuts through the prairie pothole ecosystem that is critically important nesting and migratory staging areas for many ducks, including Pintails and Mallards.[24]

Shortgrass Prairie and Mountain Plover

The South Dakota Shortgrass prairie regions, through which the Keystone pipeline passes and the proposed Keystone XL pipeline would pass, are important habitat for the Mountain Plover, proposed for listing as threatened under the Endangered Species Act.[25]

Pronghorn Antelope Habitat

The Keystone XL pipeline would traverse pronghorn antelope habitat in Montana, further fragmenting already-threatened migration routes.[26] Pronghorn are a unique American species whose movements are very sensitive to roads and human activity.

Select Rivers Threatened by United States DilBit Pipelines

Missouri River

The longest river on the continent and the route of the Lewis and Clark expedition, the Missouri is crossed by pipelines in numerous places, including by Keystone pipeline on the South Dakota-Nebraska border and the Kansas-Missouri border, by Enbridge pipelines in Missouri, and by the proposed Keystone XL pipeline in Montana, near the relatively isolated Upper Missouri River Breaks National Monument.[27]

Yellowstone River

In Montana, the proposed Keystone XL pipeline would cross the Yellowstone River, a major tributary into the Missouri River and the longest undammed river in the lower 48 states. The river is of vital use for fishermen and recreationalists, and is a major irrigation source for farmers and ranchers.[28]

Mississippi River

The Keystone pipeline crosses the Mississippi River in Missouri, near the confluence of the Mississippi and Missouri Rivers, and terminates just across the river in Illinois. Enbridge pipelines cross the northern part of the Mississippi River in Minnesota.

Kalamazoo River

In Michigan, an Enbridge pipeline crosses the Kalamazoo River which flows into Lake Michigan. A spill from this pipeline has already damaged the river ecosystem and threatened nearby communities and the Great Lakes.[29]

Red River

The Red River serves an important breeding ground for the highly endangered Interior Least Tern, which requires feeding areas with shallow waters and an abundance of small fish.[30] The proposed Keystone XL pipeline would cross the Red River on the Oklahoma-Texas border.

Neches River

The Neches River is the last river in East Texas with abundant wildlife, clean water, scenic river vistas, and forests. The proposed Keystone XL pipeline would cross the Neches River in Texas.[31]

Ensuring Our Safety

There are several steps that the United States can and should take in order to prevent future DilBit pipeline spills. These precautionary steps are essential for protecting farmland, wildlife habitat, and critical water resources—and should be put in place before rushing to approve risky infrastructure that Americans will be locked into using for decades to come.

- **Evaluate the need for new U.S. pipeline safety regulations.** Older safety standards designed for conventional oil may not provide adequate protection for communities and ecosystems in the vicinity of a DilBit pipeline. The Department of Transportation should analyze and address the potential risks associated with the transport of DilBit at the high temperatures and pressures at which those pipelines operate and put new regulations in place as necessary to address these risks.

- The oil pipeline industry should take special precautions for pipelines transporting DilBit. Until appropriate regulations are in place, oil pipeline companies should use the appropriate technology to protect against corrosion of their pipelines, to ensure that the smallest leaks can be detected in the shortest time that is technologically possible, and companies should ensure sufficient spill response assets are in place to contain a spill upon detection.

- **Improve spill response planning for DilBit pipelines.** Spill response planning for DilBit pipelines should be done through a public process in close consultation with local emergency response teams and communities.

- **New DilBit pipeline construction and development should not be considered until adequate safety regulations for DilBit pipelines are in place.** The next major proposed DilBit pipeline is TransCanada's Keystone XL pipeline. This pipeline approval process should be put on hold until PHMSA evaluates the risks of DilBit pipelines and ensures that adequate safety regulations for DilBit pipelines are in place.

- **Reduce U.S. demand for oil, especially for tar sands oil.** The United States can dramatically cut oil consumption by reinforcing existing reduction programs, such as efficiency standards for vehicles, and through new investments in alternatives to oil.

Endnotes

1. "Oil Sands Statistics 2000-2007," Canadian Association of Petroleum Producers, http://membernet.capp.ca/raw.asp?x=1&dt=NTV&e=PDF&dn=34093 (accessed January 12, 2011).

2. The United States imported 550,000 bpd of blended bitumen (DilBit, SynBit, and DilSynBit) in the 1st quarter of 2010; this does not include synthetic crude oil. *Estimated Canadian Crude Oil Exports by Type and Destination, 2010 Q1*, National Energy Board, 2010, http://www.neb-one.gc.ca/clf-nsi/rnrgynfmtn/sttstc/crdlndptrlmprdct/2010/stmtdcndncrdlxprttpdstnt2010_q1.xls (accessed January 12, 2011). The ERCB estimates that in 2009, Alberta exported 500,000 bpd of SCO (79,600 m3/day, p. 2-34) to refineries in the United States. Andy Burrowes, Rick Marsh, Marie-Anne Kirsch et al., *Alberta's Energy Reserves 2009 Supply/Demand*

Outlook 2010-2019, Calgary, Alberta: Energy Resources Conservation Board, 2010, http://www.ercb.ca/docs/products/STs/st98_current.pdf (accessed January 12, 2011).

3. Andy Burrowes, Rick Marsh, Marie-Anne Kirsch et al., *Alberta's Energy Reserves 2009 Supply/Demand Outlook 2010-2019*, Calgary, Alberta: Energy Resources Conservation Board, 2010, p. 3, http://www.ercb.ca/docs/products/STs/st98_current. pdf (accessed January 12, 2011).

4. The Keystone pipeline has a capacity of 591,000 bpd. "Keystone Pipeline Project: Project Information," TransCanada Corporation Home, TransCanada PipeLines Limited, 2010, http:// www.transcanada.com/project_information.html (accessed January 12, 2011).

5. The Alberta Clipper Pipeline has a capacity of 450,000 bpd with an ultimate capacity of up to 800,000 bpd. "Alberta Clipper," Enbridge Expansion, Enbridge, 2011, http:// www. enbridge-expansion.com/expansion/main.aspx?id=1218 (accessed January 12, 2011).

6. The Keystone XL pipeline would have a capacity of up to 900,000 bpd. "Project Home Page," U. S. Department of State: Keystone XL Pipeline Project, Entrix, Inc., July 26, 2010, http:// www.keystonepipeline-xl.state.gov (accessed January 12, 2011).

7. There are numerous cases of pipeline explosions involving NGL condensate, including the January 1, 2011 explosion of a NGL condensate line in northern Alberta ("Pengrowth investigates pipeline explosion in northern Alberta," *The Globe and Mail*, January 2, 2011, http://www.theglobeandmail.com/report-on-business/ industry-news/energy-and-resources/ pengrowth-investigates-pipeline-explosion-in-northern-alberta/article1855533/ (accessed January 12, 2011)); and the 2007 explosion of an NGL pipeline near Fort Worth Texas after it had been ruptured by a third party ("No Injuries In Parker Co. Gas Pipeline Explosion," *AP/CBS 11 News*, 12 May 2007, http://www.keiberginc.com/web_news_ les/pipeline- explosion-pr1.pdf (accessed January 12, 2011)).

8. "Material Safety Data Sheet: Natural Gas Condensates," Imperial Oil, 2002, http:// www.msdsxchange.com/english/show_msds.cfm?paramid1=2480179 (accessed January 12, 2011).

9. "Material Safety Data Sheet: Natural Gas Condensate, Petroleum," Oneok, 2009, http://www.oneokpartners.com/en/CorporateResponsibility/~/media/ONEOK/ SafetyDocs/ Natural%20Gas%20Condensate%20Petroleum.ashx (accessed January 12, 2011).

10. "Hydrogen Sulfide," Occupational Safety and Health Administration, Fact Sheet, 2005, http://www.osha.gov/OshDoc/data_Hurricane_Facts/hydrogen_sul de_fact. pdf (accessed January 12, 2011); "Material Safety Data Sheet: DilBit Cold Lake Blend," Imperial Oil, 2002, http://www.msdsxchange.com/english/show_msds. cfm?paramid1=2479752 (accessed January 12, 2011).

11. *Enbridge Line 6B 608 Pipeline Release, Marshall Michigan, Health and Safety Plan*, Enbridge, Inc., 2010, http://www.epa.gov/enbridgespill/pdfs/ nalworkplanpdfs/ enbridge_final_ healthsafety_20100819.pdf, (accessed January 12, 2011).

12. "Material Safety Data Sheet: DilBit Cold Lake Blend," Imperial Oil, 2002, http://www. msdsxchange.com/english/show_msds.cfm?paramid1=2479752 (accessed January 12, 2011).

13. Martha Stanbury et al., *Acute Health Effects of the Enbridge Oil Spill*, Lansing, MI: Michigan Department of Community Health, November 2010, http://

www.michigan.gov/documents/ mdch/enbridge_oil_spill_epi_report_with_cover_11_22_10_339101_7.pdf (accessed January 12, 2011).

14. *Toxicological Pro le for Polycyclic Aromatic Hydrocarbons,* Agency for Toxic Substances and Disease Registry, 1995, http://www.atsdr.cdc.gov/toxpro les/ tp.asp?id=122&tid=25 (accessed January 12, 2011). Benzene, Agency for Toxic Substances and Disease Registry, 1995, http://www.atsdr.cdc.gov/substances/ toxsubstance.asp?toxid=14 (accessed January 12, 2011).

15. "Athabasca Bitumen," Environment Canada, Emergencies Science and Technology Division, http://www.etc-cte.ec.gc.ca/databases/OilProperties/pdf/WEB_Athabasca_Bitumen.pdf (accessed January 12, 2011).

16. The bioaccumulation of heavy metals is well established in academic literature (see, for example, R. Vinodhini and M. Narayanan, *Bioaccumulation of heavy metals in organs of fresh water fish Cyprinus carpio (Common carp),* Int. J. Environ. Sci. Tech, 5 (2), Spring 2008, 179-182, http://www.ceers.org/ijest/issues/full/v5/n2/502005. pdf (accessed January 12, 2011)). Heavy metals are elemental in nature and cannot biodegrade and have a variety of toxic effects ("Toxicological Pro les," Agency for Toxic Substances and Disease Registry, 2010, http://www.atsdr.cdc.gov/toxpro les/ index.asp (accessed January 12, 2011)).

17. "Why is this important?" National Oceanic and Atmospheric Administration, Center of Excellence for Great Lakes and Human Health, http://www.glerl.noaa.gov/res/ Centers/ HumanHealth/ (accessed January 12, 2011).

18. "Lakehead System," Enbridge U. S. Operations, Enbridge, 2011, http://www. enbridgeus.com/Main.aspx?id=210&tmi=210&tmt=1 (accessed January 12, 2011). "Enbridge Pipelines System Configuration Quarter 4, 2010," Enbridge, 2010, http:// www.enbridge.com/DeliveringEnergy/OurPipelines/~/media/Site%20Documents/ Delivering%20Energy/2010%20 Q4%20Pipeline%20System%20Con guration.ashx (accessed January 12, 2011).

19. "Replacing River Pipeline Is a Victory," *The Times Herald,* 2010, http://www. thetimesherald.com/article/20101229/OPINION01/12290320/Replacing-river-pipeline-is-a-victory (accessed January 12, 2011).

20. "Indiana Dunes," National Park Service, 2011, http://www.nps.gov/indu/index.htm (accessed January 12, 2011).

21. "Deep Fork National Wildlife Refuge," U. S. Fish and Wildlife Service, http://www. fws.gov/refuges/pro les/index.cfm?id=21592 (accessed January 12, 2011).

22. "Topeka Shiner (Notropis Topeka)," U. S. Fish and Wildlife Service, 2011, http://ecos. fws.gov/speciesPro le/pro le/speciesProfile.action?spcode=E07R (accessed January 12, 2011).

23. Gary L. Krapu, *Sandhill Cranes and the Platte River,* pp. 103-117 in K. P. Able, ed, *Gatherings of Angels,* Chapter 7, Ithaca, NY: Cornell University Press, 1999, Jamestown, ND: Northern Prairie Wildlife Research Center Online, http://www. npwrc.usgs.gov/resource/birds/sndcrane/index.htm (accessed January 12, 2011) .

24. "Prairie Pothole Region: Level I Ducks Unlimited conservation priority area, the most important and threatened waterfowl habitat in North America," Ducks Unlimited, http://www. ducks.org/conservation/prairie-pothole-region (accessed January 12, 2011).

25. "Endangered and Threatened Wildlife and Plants; Listing the Mountain Plover as Threatened," Department of the Interior Fish and Wildlife Service,

2010, http://frwebgate.access.gpo. gov/cgi-bin/getdoc.cgi?dbname=2010_
register&docid=fr29jn10-24 (accessed January 12, 2011).

26. "Pronghorn—*Antilocapra americana*," Montana Field Guide, Montana Natural
Heritage Program and Montana Fish, Wildlife and Parks, http://FieldGuide.mt.gov/
detail_ AMALD01010.aspx (accessed January 12, 2011).

27. "Upper Missouri River Breaks National Monument," U. S. Department of Interior
Bureau of Land Management, 2010, http://www.blm.gov/mt/st/en/fo/lewistown_
field_office/ umrbnm.html (accessed January 12, 2011).

28. "About YRCDC: History," Yellowstone River Conservation District Council, 2010,
http://www.yellowstonerivercouncil.org/about.php (accessed January 12, 2011).

29. "EPA Response to Enbridge Spill in Michigan," United States Environmental
Protection Agency, 2010, http://www.epa.gov/enbridgespill/ (accessed January 12,
2011).

30. "Interior Least Tern (*Sterna antillarum athalassos*)," Texas Parks and Wildlife, 2009,
http://www.tpwd.state.tx.us/huntwild/wild/species/leasttern/ (accessed January 12,
2011).

31. Draft Environmental Impact Statement for the Keystone XL Oil Pipeline Project, U.
S. Department of State, 2010, p. 3.3-18.

13

The Trump Administration Poses a Threat to the Planet

Michael Ware

Vermont-based socialist and climate justice activist Michael Ware writes for sites like the Socialist Worker *and the* International Socialist Review.

After assuming office, President Donald Trump and his administration wasted no time pursuing an anti-environmental agenda, according to the following viewpoint by writer Michael Ware. He warns that climate change denial, pushing through the Dakota Access Pipeline, and economic nationalism could very well spur environmental destruction and abandon any progress towards battling global warming.

Donald Trump's executive orders for a ban on Muslims entering the U.S. and for building a border wall provoked the most visible and immediate responses of the early days of his presidency.

But his moves to restart construction of the Keystone XL and Dakota Access pipelines and the new administration's censorship of government workers and federally funded scientists regarding climate change were a shot across the bow of the environmental movement.

Upon taking office, Twittler and his henchmen directed federal agencies to cease public communication that wasn't vetted by the

"Trump's "America First" Puts the Planet Last," by Michael Ware, SocialistWorker.org, February 9, 2017. Reprinted by Permission.

new administration, effectively putting a gag order on any talk about climate change or scientific research that contradicts the administration's taste for "alternative facts."

The Badlands National Park Twitter account defied the ban, issuing unspeakable truths like "The Pre-Industrial concentration of carbon dioxide in the atmosphere was 280 parts per million (ppm). As of December 2016, 404.93ppm." The account has since been reigned in and the tweets deleted.

This week, the new administration scored a victory when the U.S. Army Corps of Engineers, bowing to an order from Trump, reversed its denial of an easement needed to complete a section of the Dakota Access Pipeline running under the Missouri River. The Army Corps not only abandoned plans to wait for an environment impact study, but rushed through approval so drilling could start in 24 hours—making it harder for the Standing Rock Sioux Tribe to take action in court.

All that is a taste of things to come in a Trump administration where many appointees are deeply committed to climate change denial, the oil and gas industry or aggressive U.S. militarism—and usually all three at the same time.

Add this to Trump's economic nationalism, and you have a virtual guarantee that the U.S. government will lead a charge to abandon the limited progress made in combatting global warming, drop enforcement of environmental regulations and the already weak Paris Climate Agreement, and ramp up production of domestic oil, fracked gas, shale oil, coal and even Canadian tar sands.

Trump's newly approved Secretary of State Rex Tillerson is the former CEO of ExxonMobil. Tillerson has a cozy relationship with Russia, economically, one of the world's major energy exporters. Tillerson will be in a position to green light projects such as the extension of the previously halted Keystone XL pipeline—and to reinforce a foreign policy historically focused on dominating the Middle East and the flow of oil around the globe.

Millions of acres of federal lands, national parks and seashores will be supervised by Interior Secretary Ryan Zinke, who thinks that man-made climate change is unproven science, and in any case, that energy independence comes first.

The incoming head of the Environmental Protection Agency (EPA), Scott Pruitt, spent his time as the Oklahoma Attorney General trying to sue the EPA out of existence. Though he largely failed and won't be able to destroy the agency overnight, he will likely help the Trump administration cut enforcement budgets for vital regulations pertaining to clean water and industrial pollution.

As Energy Secretary, former Texas Gov. and all-around idiot Rick Perry will be responsible for the U.S. nuclear arsenal as well as many renewable energy initiatives. As for climate change, Perry once said, "It's all one contrived phony mess that is falling apart under its own weight."

Defense Secretary James "Mad Dog" Mattis likes shooting Afghan men, yet Bernie Sanders and every Senate Democrat except Kirsten Gillibrand voted to confirm his nomination. With Trump promising to drastically increase the budget Mad Dog oversees, we should assume the military's consumption of 100 million barrels of oil per year will grow—and will force other countries to do the same.

And then there's the rabidly neoliberal, anti-regulation Republican Congress, so don't expect any checks and balances there.

The Paris climate agreement at the 2015 UN summit at least popularized the relatively conservative idea that global temperatures cannot increase more than 2 degrees Centigrade without risking severe environmental disruption.

But at a time when global carbon emissions should be decreasing by 10 percent each year, Donald Trump's will throw any progress into reverse.

Trump is determined to ramp up production after Barack Obama's "all of the above" energy strategy. But beyond that, U.S. protectionism and fossil-fuel dependency will compel other nations to carry out similar measures. As Benjamin Sanderson and Reto Knutti wrote in *Nature*:

> The exit of the U.S. from the Paris Agreement, or the failure of the U.S. to meet its targets, would likely present severe challenges for the international community to meet its emissions goals. Legally U.S. inaction does not affect other countries' obligations, but the fear that others would free-ride was one of the main hurdles in over 20 years of climate negotiations. In their initial response, China indicated that U.S. plans would not affect their mitigation efforts, but India said they could. So it is at least plausible that other countries would also reduce their efforts, and it is worth exploring the consequences.

Chinese President Xi Jinping has urged the U.S. to stay in the Paris climate pact. Lacking significant fossil fuel resources itself, China announced that it would fill the role of world leader in renewable energy development abandoned by the U.S., promising to invest $361 billion in new projects. It will need these developments if Trump's administration succeeds, with or without an alliance with Russia, in disrupting China's access to oil imports.

This is another reason—beyond the individual fanaticism of Trump and close advisers like alt-righter Steve Bannon—why the new administration is so determined to double down on fossil fuel production, deregulation, protectionism and corporate tax breaks. These are a backward, but sadly not irrational, response to the U.S. sluggish growth and America's relative decline as the unchallenged global superpower.

Trump isn't the first president to push a goal of "energy independence."

George W. Bush and Dick Cheney used the pretext of the September 11 attacks to launch a "war on terror" designed to reshape the Middle East and tighten America's grip on the region's oil resources, at the expense of Russia, China and Iran.

But the Bush Doctrine was undermined by the disastrous U.S. occupation of Iraq. By 2007, a Republican administration filled with oil and gas executives hesitantly embraced renewable energy with the Energy Independence and Security Act.

Under Barack Obama, the Democrats continued the pursuit of energy independence with their all-of-the-above policy that led to a rapid increase in U.S. oil and fracked gas production. The oil-producing nations of the OPEC cartel refused to cut production, hoping to undermine the new glut in the U.S.

Oil prices plunged for several years, throwing countries that export oil and other raw materials into recession or worse. While many U.S. fracking operations went under, the industry has largely stabilized, due to advances in the mix of chemicals, sand and water used to extract gas and contaminate your groundwater. Meanwhile, Trump's threatened protectionist trade measures could make oil prices and supplies even more unpredictable.

This backdrop explains the urgency around completing DAPL and Keystone XL. The administration wants to increase domestic production to lessen the impact of recent production cuts by OPEC, which partially supply U.S. imports of 10 million barrels per day. That could raise prices and profits for U.S. oil producers if they are able to sustain production—and retool refineries, many of which are used to processing heavier grades of oil from Venezuela.

The OPEC production cut could fall apart if the U.S. increases production and even exports what it can't refine. Though unlikely, another scenario would be for OPEC to react to U.S. protectionism and escalating threats with a replay of its 1970s embargo, which tipped the global economy into a major recession.

Republicans will try to dismantle Obama-era energy initiatives—for example, answering the auto industry's prayers by repealing new EPA regulations mandating a fleet average fuel efficiency of 54.5 miles per gallon by 2025. Actually, everyone acknowledges that the Obama standards is 40 miles per gallon under real driving conditions—the difference is a perfect metaphor for Obama's meager legacy on climate issues.

The environmental movement will be tempted to wax nostalgic for the Obama years, but we can't afford to ignore the reality of what took place over the past eight years. Behind his seductive rhetoric was a cynical president who countered every restriction on polluters or nod to renewable energy with a quiet embrace of fracking, "clean coal," Arctic drilling and imperialism.

In the aftermath of the Occupy movement and the Arab Spring, the global environmental movement grew more confrontational and shifted the debate around climate change.

Though not strong enough to force a more substantial shift away from fossil fuels, protest and organizing clearly proved to be more effective than decades of lobbying. That was the lesson of the direct action movement that stopped an Obama administration intent on green-lighting the Keystone XL. Plus, there was the Standing Rock struggle, which won unity among Native American tribes and solidarity from masses of Non-Native supporters.

That struggle will have to be revived following the capitulation of the Army Corps of Engineers on granting a permit to complete DAPL. The process will be complicated by a debate in Standing Rock itself over whether the camps should continue or the focus should move to the courts.

There's more for the climate justice movement to look forward to in the coming months.

One date to save is the March for Science, set for Washington, D.C., on Earth Day, April 22. Like many outbreaks of protest against Trump, this event began with a social media post among a group of scientists. "We hope to humanize scientists as approachable members of our communities, and to draw attention to dangerous trends in the politicization of science," noted march organizer Jonathan Berman, a University of Texas Health Science Center postdoctoral fellow.

One week later, the organizers behind the 2014 People's Climate March in New York City have called for a similar People's Climate March on Washington on April 29.

Beyond these, the boundaries around environmental struggles are blurring and breaking down under the pressure of Trump and Bannon's shock and awe opening days. The struggles to stop pipeline construction and any fossil fuel infrastructure locking in high carbon emissions share a common enemy with people fighting to save abortion rights, end the ban on Muslims or stop the border wall with Mexico.

With a new generation finding its political voice in the struggles against Trumpism, the questions that need to be answered will broaden out as well: Is Trump an aberration, an outgrowth of a capitalist system in decline, or both? Where does our power to resist lie? How do we organize ourselves beyond big marches and events?

The Trump nightmare and the wave of struggle it has produced present both a horrific scenario of accelerated environmental destruction and an opportunity for multiple movements to grow and support each other. The old slogan "An injury to one is an injury to all" has never made more sense.

14

Canadian Economic Prosperity Depends on Oil Sands

Shawn McCarthy

Shawn McCarthy is based in Ottawa, Canada, and reports on global energy issues for The Globe and Mail, including oil and gas production and refining, the development of new technologies, and the business implications of climate-change regulations.

Commercial quality oil produced from Alberta, Canada's tarry bitumen is big business for the country. As global energy reporter Shawn McCarthy explains in the following viewpoint, many are banking on this, their largest export industry, to expand into the growing market of Asia. This fifty-plus year old industry has seen its ups and downs through time. Debate across Canada continues with supporters and detractors throughout the nation.

Everything about Alberta's oil sands is huge—from the sheer scale of the 170-billion-barrel resource in the ground, to the two-storey trucks that haul bitumen ore in the mines, to the $30-billion per year in capital investment to expand the flow of crude.

The industry was born 50 years ago with the largest single private investment made in Canada to that date, a $250-million bet by a forerunner of today's Suncor Energy Inc. The bid to produce commercial grade oil from the tarry bitumen that seeped through

"Why the Oil Sands Matter to Every Canadian," by Shawn McCarthy, The Globe and Mail Inc, May 25, 2017. Reprinted by Permission.

the muskeg of Northern Alberta was dubbed the "biggest gamble in history." It was unlike any oil production that had been done—using massive mining and manufacturing machinery rather than the drilling rigs that coaxed crude from the ground in Texas and Saudi Arabia.

In the half-century since, oil sands producers have overcome the challenges of subarctic climate and wrenching oil price crashes. Now they are facing equally enormous tests: the need to access new markets and to mitigate their heavy environmental footprint.

Failure to meet those tests could slam the brakes on ambitious plans to double oil sands production over the next decade to four million barrels per day.

At stake is Canada's largest export industry, one whose economic clout extends far beyond Alberta to labour markets on the East Coast, to Toronto's financial district, and to a supply chain that extends across North America. Industry proponents argue Canada's national prosperity depends on the oil industry's access to new markets, especially in fast-growing Asia.

But that claim is hugely contentious. Supporters tend to exaggerate the economic benefits of the oil sands outside Alberta's borders. And it is unwise to depend on the industry for the country's economic well-being unless it can be made environmentally sustainable—a costly effort in a sector where high costs are already problematic.

Certainly, the battle to construct much-needed pipelines is fraught with difficulty, running through a minefield of environmental and aboriginal opposition. Proposed pipelines span the breadth of Canada: crossing mountain ranges to terminals on the West Coast where people who play on and make their living from the sea are loath to have more crude-bearing supertankers plying their waters; or heading east to the Atlantic Ocean past towns where Ontarians and Quebeckers often see risk but little reward.

Every oil-company executive in Calgary—certainly any one of them watching the current slump in oil prices—knows that today's success can be fleeting. Producers of natural gas saw prices plunge from $12 (U.S.) per thousand cubic feet in 2008 to below $3 (U.S.) last year, and see little room for optimism. Oil-patch veterans remember the bust of the mid-1980s, which brought early oil sands construction to a halt and threatened the very viability of Fort McMurray's fledgling industry.

Yet now that the oil sands dominate Canada's largest export industry and draw such international opprobrium, it is easy to forget the visionary beginnings of the industry.

Early explorers like Alexander Mackenzie remarked on the tarry bitumen that was seen oozing out of the ground on the banks of the Athabasca River. A century later, a member of a delegation that had come to negotiate a native land treaty noted the region "is stored with a substance of great economic value."

But it was the diligence of a chemist from Georgetown, Ontario, Karl Clark, that proved its commercial value. Dr. Clark joined the Alberta Scientific and Industrial Research Council in 1921, when the province was only 16 years old. He spent his career researching how to use hot water and chemicals to produce commercial-grade crude from the bitumen. He helped perfect the process in the 1950s at a pilot plant at Bitumount, located 90 kilometres north of Fort McMurray. But the big strike at Leduc in 1947 shifted attention to conventional oil, and by 1958, Bitumount fell into disrepair.

Two men kept the dream alive: Social Credit Premier Ernest Manning and Pittsburgh industrialist J. Howard Pew, president of Sun Oil Co. Manning never lost sight of the economic potential that the oil sands held for his province.

Pew—whose family trust is now a major funder of some anti-oil sands environmental groups—invested heavily in Great Canadian Oil Sands Ltd., the forerunner of Suncor. The two men attended the official opening of the company's first plant near Fort McMurray in 1967. Even as Expo 67 was putting Canada on the international map, the Alberta Premier declared that "no other event in Canada's centennial year is more important or significant."

Since that bold beginning, the oil sands have seen boom and bust. The Arab oil embargo of 1973 drove up world oil prices and breathed life into the capital-intensive tar sands. The Iranian revolution generated even more enthusiasm, as Albertans became known in the rest of Canada as "blue-eyed sheiks." But what goes up too fast tends to come down with a thud. And when oil prices collapsed—hitting $10 (U.S.) per barrel in 1986—the sector went into a slump that was to last nearly 20 years.

In the mid-1990s, with oil prices at depressed levels, the Liberal government of Jean Chrétien had to provide tax breaks to rescue the industry, in particular the two major oil sands producers, Suncor and Syncrude Canada Ltd. It wasn't until international crude prices began to soar in 2003—reflecting war in the Middle East and the rise in China's demand—that the oil sands sector found firm economic footing and expansion began in earnest.

A popular bumper sticker from the 1980s sums up the make-hay-while-the-sun-shines mentality: "Please God, let there be another oil boom. I promise not to piss it all away next time." And while the collapse of international prices was a critical reason for Alberta's 1980s bust, Ottawa and its interventionist National Energy Program will always share the blame in the minds of many Albertans. And there is an abiding fear in Calgary that Ottawa will again remove the punch bowl, spurred on this time by climate concerns rather than economic nationalism.

So far, the oil sands producers have largely escaped the climate lash. Alberta set some modest standards and charges a small levy when producers exceed their targets. But despite numerous promises to do so, the Harper government has so far refused to impose federal measures to control greenhouse gas (GHG) emissions from the oil sands. Based on the current production forecast, the sector will see its emissions grow by 56 megatonnes by 2020, offsetting all the reductions gained by phasing out coal-fired electricity in Ontario and lower outputs in other provinces. In the 2009 climate summit at Copenhagen, Harper pledged that Canada would reduce its emissions by 17 per cent from 2005 levels by 2020, a commitment that will be impossible to meet given the expected growth in the oil sands.

Indeed, the Harper government has spent considerable political capital defending the industry. Harper has strained relations between his government and the administration of President Barack Obama, which has delayed a decision on the proposed Keystone XL pipeline.

The Conservatives have overhauled—"gutted" according to critics—environmental regulations, while condemning industry opponents as "radicals."

Both Harper and Alberta's new premier, Jim Prentice, now insist Canada can only impose additional GHG regulations on the oil industry if the U.S. hits its booming crude producers with similar regulations. But Obama is engaged in a fierce battle with Republicans and the coal industry over his plan to impose carbon regulations on the coal-fired power sector, which is by far the largest source of CO_2 emissions in the United States. Waiting for the Americans to deal with carbon emissions in their oil sector would delay Canadian action for years. Pressure will grow for Canada to table a national emissions-reduction strategy as countries work to achieve an international agreement at a United Nations-sponsored climate summit in Paris next year.

And with a federal election expected next year, the industry could well face a new government in Ottawa that would be more determined than the current one is to establish a national plan to reduce carbon emissions by reining in the oil sands. Greg Stringham, vice-president of the Canadian Association of Petroleum Producers, acknowledges that the oil sands' emissions will increase so long as production expands at projected rates.

Some companies have made progress in reducing their emissions of carbon dioxide per barrel of oil produced. Imperial Oil Ltd. says bitumen from its new Kearl mine has a lifetime GHG output roughly equivalent to conventional oil, while Cenovus Energy Inc. is experimenting with solvents to reduce the steam needed to extract bitumen when companies employ steam-assisted gravity drainage techniques. Reducing the amount of steam generated by burning natural gas would cut CO_2 emissions.

Stringham says innovation could bring down emissions-per-barrel by up to 20 per cent over the next 15 years, but that overall emissions would still head sharply higher due to production growth. The industry recognizes the world will need to transition away from high-carbon fuel. But the producers believe the transition will take decades, and that Canadians—and a growing number of people around the world—will need oil to fuel their modern lifestyles.

Environmentalists argue the climate can't wait. Some, like U.S. climate scientist James Hansen, say rising oil sands production would mean "game over for the climate." Others take a more measured view, proposing a stiff carbon tax that would slow but not stop production growth. "Ninety-nine per cent of environmentalists out there are not pushing for elimination of oil or the oil sands any time soon," says Rick Smith, executive director of the Broadbent Institute, a left-of-centre think tank. "What we need is a national discussion on how we're going to reduce carbon pollution in this country, and how everyone will do their fair share."

Making the oil sands cleaner costs money—and they already rank among the world's most expensive places to get crude. Major projects have been cancelled by international companies like Norway's Statoil SA and France's Total SA, which cited poor economics. The Calgary-based Canadian Energy Research Institute (CERI) estimates that a new mine would need an oil price of $105 (U.S.) a barrel to make a reasonable return, while a typical in-situ project would require a price of $85. Piling on more costs for environmental reasons could drive away badly needed investment. "Those types of social-licence issues could make the oil sands uneconomic if you added on enough of them," says CERI president Peter Howard, whose institute recently produced a report on the "uncertainties" facing the oil sands sector.

While the industry has successfully fended off tougher carbon regulations for now, it is facing an uphill battle on pipelines. If they're not built, climate activists may achieve indirectly what they couldn't do in a head-on battle. CERI forecasts that a failure to win approval for major pipeline projects would slash 1.8 million barrels per day from anticipated oil sands production in 2030. Because the crude would be trapped in North America, producers would have to sell it at a deep discount, costing them $20 (U.S.) on every barrel they sell.

Indeed, as they sought to "decarbonize" the economy, environmentalists turned their spotlight on not just the oil sands but also on its pipelines. BP PLC's Gulf of Mexico disaster and Enbridge Inc's ugly spill on Michigan's Kalamazoo River illustrated local risks. On top of that, First Nations communities across Canada are determined to exert more power over development on their traditional lands, and pipeline companies face lengthy court battles to determine whether, once armed with approval from the National Energy Board, they can override aboriginal objections. That legal landscape has created tremendous uncertainty for the industry, says Robert Johnston, chief executive officer at Eurasia Group, a New York-based political-risk firm. "It used to be the NEB process was difficult but once you got that, you had a social licence to operate," Johnston says. "But that seems to be no longer the case. Now, once you get your NEB permit, the real negotiations begin. That's a very new and very complicated, difficult business model because it is not clear what the exit model is. How do you know when you have a social licence?"

What would be lost if the oil sands produces 3.7 million barrels a day at $70 a barrel, rather than five million barrels at $90? In its report on the future of the oil sands, CERI repeats a common refrain heard from the industry and the politicians that support it: "Canada's future economic prosperity depends on its ability to provide reliable infrastructure to allow Canadian energy resources to fuel Asian economic growth at world market prices." The Alberta government says the sector supports the jobs of 112,000 Canadians outside the province, a figure it says will grow to 500,000 in 25 years. In a 2012 report, the Conference Board of Canada forecast the oil sands sector would generate $79.4-billion in federal and provincial revenues from 2012 to 2035. Oil sands jobs for out-of-province workers—mainly from Atlantic Canada—have resulted in a significant drop in unemployment in their provinces and a flow of money back home. The sector "certainly does have positive effects to the Canadian economy as a whole," Toronto-Dominion Bank economist Craig Alexander says. "There are knock-on effects nationally, but there is no question the provinces that benefit most are the provinces where the energy resources reside."

A trickier question is whether the boom in the oil sands has had negative impacts outside Alberta. Former Ontario premier Dalton McGuinty once mused about those potential costs and faced such a storm of outrage that he quickly backtracked. But some economists still argue that the rapid rise in the Canadian dollar between 2003 and 2008—and again after a recessionary slump in 2009—reflect the country's status as a "petro currency." The oil-fuelled increase in the loonie undermined the export-oriented manufacturing sector centred in Ontario and Quebec, argue Bank of America economists Emanuella Enenajor and Ian Gordon in a recent report titled "Canada's Dutch Disease."

It's been an ongoing debate: In 2012, then Bank of Canada governor Mark Carney rejected the Dutch disease argument as "overly simplistic," arguing rising commodity prices benefit the Canadian economy and that the higher dollar was only partly responsible for the decline in manufacturing. But the industry tends to overstate the benefits for the rest of the country, says Matthew Mendelsohn, director of the Mowat Centre, a Toronto-based think tank. "The growth in the oil sands has created some opportunities in Ontario and elsewhere," says Mendelsohn, a former deputy minister in Ontario. "But it has also been the primary driver of increases in our emissions—which we will have to pay for at some time—and it has driven up the dollar exceptionally and created volatility in our currency, which has hurt manufacturing significantly in Central Canada."

The oil sands debate reveals a balkanized and deeply polarized Canada. In a country where one province discriminates against another's winemakers, it's small wonder the biggest question on interprovincial crude pipelines is: What's in it for me? The

Harper government vilifies pipeline opponents as radicals bent on undermining the national interest, while environmentalists paint the Prime Minister as public enemy No. 1 on climate change. The loudest voices proclaim: "Let her rip" or "Shut her down." Somewhere in between, there's a path that weighs the economic benefits against the environmental costs, takes into account the rights of First Nations and the need for a competitive industry, and deploys capital into 40-year projects that won't be stranded as the world moves to a low-carbon economy.

15

Offshore Oil Production Could Alleviate Poverty for Indigenous People

Bill Flowers

Bill Flowers is a resident of Amherst, Nova Scotia, and a member of the Labrador Inuit community. Retired from public service, he works as a consultant to First Nations.

For more than 45 years, various individuals in Canada have been talking about the poverty issue among the nation's indigenous people. Various suggestions have been made to attack this problem, including government-sponsored programs. In the following viewpoint from Bill Flowers, an Inuit writer from Nova Scotia, a case is made for the management and development of Canada's offshore hydrocarbon resources being turned over to indigenous communities.

If I had to count the number of times I have heard that we need to "lift Indigenous people out of poverty" and "make Indigenous people equal and productive partners in Canada's social and economic fabric," I just would not know where or when to begin. It seems I have been hearing similar sentiments going back more than 45 years.

We heard it from politicians dating back to the Supreme Court's decision in *Calder* in 1973.

We heard it from the Royal Commission on Aboriginal Peoples in 1996.

"An Offshore Deal for Indigenous People?" by Bill Flowers, Institute for Research on Public Policy, February 20, 2017. Reprinted by Permission.

We heard it from Prime Minister Stephen Harper in the government's apology on residential schools on June 11, 2008.

We heard it during the Truth and Reconciliation Commission process and in the commission's calls to action in 2015.

And we are especially hearing it now in what appears to be the Liberal government's desire to open nation-to-nation relationships with Indigenous peoples and to implement the United Nations Declaration on the Rights of Indigenous Peoples.

This is just a smattering of what has, up to now, proven to be nothing more than lip service.

Indigenous people still lag behind the rest of the country in educational achievements. Many Indigenous people live in overcrowded homes in communities that lack the infrastructure to provide safe drinking water to their people. It is a well-known fact that the rate of incarceration of Indigenous persons in our prisons far exceeds that of the non-Indigenous population, as does the proportion of Indigenous children in foster homes.

It is time we recognized that poverty is at the root of the social malaise in which many of our Indigenous people find themselves. Most Indigenous people in this country are not as lucky as some of their western First Nations cousins, who are sitting on oil and gas reserves and have found themselves in a bargaining position that would be the envy of many. And more power to them. The result in places like Fort McKay First Nation in Alberta—which is prospering from the oil sands service businesses it has built—is perhaps what meaningful partnerships are supposed to look like *looking at it from a distance.*

It is time to take a new approach to how we create wealth in Indigenous communities. Despite the many efforts to roll out various government economic development programs, which support projects like building service stations and hotels, what we as a country need to do is turn our minds to how we attract new investment to Indigenous communities.

The federal government has a policy that deals with addressing past wrongs: cases where First Nations have lost land through, among other things, the unlawful surrender of reserve land. Many of the events that gave rise to today's land claims happened well over a century ago. The policy deals with the settlement of specific claims. In the Atlantic region of Canada, the process tends to take years, sometimes decades, to resolve and usually involves financial compensation determined by actuarial calculations. It also often involves the replacement of lost land by allowing the First Nations to acquire new land to add to their reserves.

Canada's offshore hydrocarbon resources hold huge potential for growth, which up to now has been the domain of the oil companies. Canadians should start thinking about the ownership of those lands and the benefits that flow from them in a different way, starting with the creation of a new deal for First Nations.

I can hear the arguments before a discussion like this even gets started. People will say that the offshore areas are not traditional Indian lands, nor have Indigenous people traditionally played a role in the development of offshore oil and gas. Let's look at it another way. The whole industry of offshore oil exploration and production is anything but traditional and is a new economic driver, particularly in eastern Canada. What long traditional history of activity does Canada or its provinces have in the offshore that entitles the government to control land leases and choose who has access to them? Canada was not involved in offshore oil and gas at the time of contact—that is, when Euro-immigrants landed on the shores of North America, 500 years ago.

We need to consider how to involve more Indigenous communities in the benefits associated with oil exploration and production. The place to start is to set aside lands in the offshore known to hold significant resources for willing Indigenous communities to control so that they become the authorities negotiating with the oil companies for exploration and drilling rights. What could possibly be wrong with that idea?

Today the government tells First Nations that they are free to find land for economic development purposes, adjacent to their reserves. (Often that is difficult. Try finding high-potential land in New Brunswick that is not already controlled by a major entity!) Rather than that approach, let's see how the government can work with Indigenous communities to acquire land in the offshore so they can work with the oil companies to develop arrangements that will see revenue-sharing, employment and other benefits. This approach would create sustainable, lasting resources for their communities. It is a way to share the wealth.

In 1978, Minister of Fisheries and Oceans Roméo LeBlanc reserved three deep-sea shrimp fishing licences for fishermen's organizations in Labrador. Much of the newly discovered resource was off the Labrador coast. New entities were born in Labrador, owned and controlled by the fishermen, and the early days saw a plethora of foreign and domestic interests travelling to Labrador to meet with fishermen to make deals. And many deals were made. People new to this fishery became trained and employed on the vessels in the offshore fishery. Money began flowing to the companies that the fishermen owned, by way of licence fees, and that allowed the community-based companies to invest in other ventures in the community.

In southern Labrador, for example, new fish plants were built, new resources harvested and new jobs created. Additionally, as a result of those licence fees, the people created their own credit union, which has been highly successful. So with the stroke of a pen, and not insignificant vision, LeBlanc transformed many coastal communities by creating these new opportunities and diversifying an economy that benefited Indigenous people.

Yet there were those voices that said to Indigenous fishermen, "You people have no place in this fishery. You have no tradition in it. You are babes in the woods. Leave this to the big boys!" Well, Labrador fishermen were persistent and held onto LeBlanc's vision. They continue to be players in this offshore fishery, whether the "big boys" like it or not.

To help "lift Indigenous people out of poverty," Canada can do something similar with respect to the management of offshore oil lands and resources. All it takes is political guts, visionary leadership and an open mind, as Roméo LeBlanc demonstrated in the late 1970s.

16

Less Energy Consumption Is the Answer

Richard Heinberg

Richard Heinberg is a senior fellow at the Post Carbon Institute. Heinberg has written numerous articles and essays, and lectured on issues dealing with energy and climate to a wide array of audiences. He most recently co-authored the book, Our Renewable Future: Laying the Path for One Hundred Percent Clean Energy *in 2016.*

In the following viewpoint, Post Carbon Institute essayist Richard Heinberg engages in a point by point debate and analysis of renewable energy sources and the issues surrounding their current usage—along with weighing the transition to a world situation beyond the use of carbon energy sources. Key concepts and possible outcomes are dissected, and the inevitable conclusion reached by the author points to a necessary decrease of energy consumption.

Folks who pay attention to energy and climate issues are regularly treated to two competing depictions of society's energy options.* On one hand, the fossil fuel industry claims that its products deliver unique economic benefits, and that giving up coal, oil, and natural gas in favor of renewable energy sources like solar and wind will entail sacrifice and suffering. Saving the climate may not be worth the trouble, they say, unless we can find affordable ways to capture and sequester carbon as we continue burning fossil fuels.

"Our Renewable Future," by Richard Heinberg, Post Carbon Institute, January 21, 2015. Reprinted by Permission.

On the other hand, at least some renewable energy proponents tell us there is plenty of wind and sun, the fuel is free, and the only thing standing between us and a climate-protected world of plentiful, sustainable, "green" energy, jobs, and economic growth is the political clout of the coal, oil, and gas industries.

Which message is right? Will our energy future be fueled by fossils (with or without carbon capture technology), or powered by abundant, renewable wind and sunlight? Does the truth lie somewhere between these extremes—that is, does an "all of the above" energy future await us? Or is our energy destiny located in a Terra Incognita that neither fossil fuel promoters nor renewable energy advocates talk much about? As maddening as it may be, the latter conclusion may be the one best supported by the facts.

If that uncharted land had a motto, it might be, "How we use energy is as important as how we get it."

Unburnable Fossils and Intermittent Electricity

Let's start with the claim that giving up coal, oil, and gas will hurl us back to the Stone Age. It's true that fossil fuels have offered extraordinary economic benefits. The cheap, concentrated, and portable energy stored in these remarkable substances opened the way, during the past couple of centuries, for industrial expansion on a scale previously inconceivable. Why not just continue burning fossil fuels, then? Over the long term that is simply not an option, for two decisive reasons.

First, burning fossil fuels is changing the climate to such a degree, and at such a pace, that economic as well as ecological ruin may ensue within the lifetimes of today's schoolchildren. The science is in: either we go cold turkey on our coal, oil, and gas addictions, or we risk raising the planet's temperature to a level incompatible with the continued existence of civilization.

Second, these are depleting, non-renewable sources of energy. We have harvested them using the low-hanging fruit principle, which means that further increments of extraction will entail rising costs (for example, the oil industry's costs for exploration and production have recently been soaring at nearly 11 percent per year) as well as worsening environmental risks. This problem has been sneaking up on us over the last ten years, as sputtering conventional oil and natural gas production set the stage for the Great Recession and the expensive (and environmentally destructive) practices of "fracking" and tar sands mining. Despite the recent plunge in oil prices the fossil fuel party is indeed over. Sooner or later the stark reality of declining fossil energy availability will rivet everyone's attention: we are overwhelmingly dependent on these fuels for nearly everything we eat, consume, use, and trade, and—as Americans started to learn in the 1970s as a result of a couple nasty oil shocks—the withdrawal symptoms are killer.

So while fossil fuel promoters are right in saying that coal, oil, and gas are essential to our current economy, what they omit mentioning is actually more crucial if we care how our world will look more than a few years into the future.

Well then, are the most enthusiastic of the solar and wind boosters correct in claiming that renewable energy sources are ready to substitute for coal, oil, and gas quickly enough and in sufficient quantity to keep the global economy growing? There's a hitch here, which critics are only too quick to point out. We've designed our energy consumption patterns to take advantage of controllable inputs. Need more power? If you're relying on coal for energy, just shovel more fuel into the boiler. But solar and wind are different: they are available on Nature's terms, not ours. Sometimes the sun is shining or the wind is blowing, sometimes not. Energy geeks have a vocabulary to describe this—they say solar and wind power are intermittent, variable, stochastic, or chaotic.

There are ways of buffering this variability: we can store energy from renewable sources with batteries or flywheels, or pump water uphill so as to recapture its potential energy later when it flows back downstream; or we can build a massive super-grid with robustly redundant generating capacity so that, when sun and wind aren't available in one region, another region can cover demand throughout the entire interconnected system. But these strategies cost money and energy, and add layers of complexity and vulnerability to what is already the largest machine ever built (i.e., the power grid).

Crucially, a recent study by Weissbach *et al.* compared the full-lifecycle energy economics of various types of power plants and found that once the intermittency of solar and wind energy is buffered by storage technologies, these sources become far less efficient than coal, natural gas, or nuclear plants; indeed, once storage is added, solar and wind fall "below the economical threshold" of long-term viability, regardless of the falling dollar price of panels and turbines themselves. The problem lies in the fact that the amount of energy embodied in the full generation-storage system cannot be repaid, with a substantial energy profit, by that system over its lifetime. Recent operational studies of solar PV systems in Spain and Australia have come to similar conclusions.

Another way to deal with variability is *demand management,* which can take a variety of forms (I'll be discussing some of those later in a fair amount of detail). These all, by definition, mean changing the ways we *use* energy. But for the moment let's stay with the subject of energy *supply.*

Early increments of solar and wind power are easy and cheap to integrate into the existing electricity distribution system because power from gas-fired peaking plants can quickly (literally, by the minute) be ramped up or down to accommodate these new, small, variable inputs while also matching changing overall demand levels. In this case, the price of wind and solar energy gets counted as just the immediate cost of building, installing, and maintaining turbines and panels. And, as the *New York Times* recently noted, the price of electricity from renewables (counted this way) is now often competitive with electricity from fossil fuels. On this basis, solar and wind are disruptive technologies: they're getting cheaper while fossil fuels can only grow costlier. This one clear economic advantage of renewable energy—free "fuel" in the forms of sunlight and wind—is decisive, as Germany is now seeing with falling wholesale electricity prices (though retail prices are rising due to feed-in tariffs that require the utility industry to pay above-market prices for renewable electricity).

But as electricity from variable renewables makes up a larger and larger proportion of all power generated, the requirements for energy storage technologies, capacity redundancy, and grid upgrades will inevitably climb; indeed, beyond a certain point, the scale of needed investment is likely to explode. Grid managers tend to say that the inflection point arrives when solar and wind power provide about 30 percent of total electricity demand, though one computer model suggests it could be put off until 80 percent market penetration is achieved. (For two contrasting views on the question of how expensive and difficult intermittency makes the renewables transition—from renewable energy optimists Jacobson and Delucchi on one hand, and from "The Simpler Way" advocate Ted Trainer on the other—see a highly informative peer-reviewed exchange here, here, and here.) The looming need for investment in storage and grid upgrades is part of the reason some electric utility companies are starting to wage war against renewables (another part is that net metering puts utilities at a disadvantage relative to solar homeowners; still another is simply that fossil fuel interests hate competition from solar and wind on general principle). As solar panels get cheaper, more homes and businesses install them; this imposes intermittency-smoothing costs on utility companies, which then raise retail prices to ratepayers. The latter then have even more of an incentive to install self-contained, battery-backed solar and abandon the grid altogether, leading to a utility "death spiral."

Yet renewable energy technologies currently require fossil fuels for their construction and deployment, so in effect they are functioning as a parasite on the back of the older energy infrastructure. The question is, can they survive the death of their host?

The Liquid Fuels Substitution Quandary

So far, we've talked only about electricity. The power generation sector arguably represents the easiest phase of the overall energy transition (since alternative technologies do exist, even if they're problematic)—but only about 22 percent of global energy is consumed in the form of electrical power; in the US the figure is 33 percent. Our biggest single energy source is oil, which fuels nearly all transportation. Transport is central to trade, which in turn is the beating heart of the global market economy. Oil also fuels the agricultural sector, and eating is fairly important to most of us. Of the three main fossil fuels, oil is showing the most immediate signs of depletion, and renewable options for replacing it are fairly dismal.

It is possible to electrify much of our transportation, and electric cars are now decorating showrooms. But they have a minuscule market share and, at the current growth rate, will take many decades to oust conventional gasoline-fueled automobiles (some analysts believe that growth rate will soon increase dramatically). In any case, batteries do not do well in large, heavy vehicles. The reason has to do with energy density: an electric battery typically is able to store and deliver only about 0.1 to 0.5 megajoules of energy per kilogram; thus, compared to gasoline or diesel (at 44 to 48 MJ/kg), it is very heavy in relation to its energy output. Some breakthroughs in battery storage density and price appear to be on the horizon, but even with these improvements the problem remains: the theoretical maximum energy storage for batteries (about 5 MJ/kg) is still far below the energy density of oil. Neither long-haul trucking nor container shipping is ever likely to be electrified on any significant scale, and electric airliners are simply a non-starter.

The promise of biofuels as a direct substitute for petroleum was widely touted a decade ago, but we hear much less on that score these days. It turns out that enormous subsidies are needed because the processes for producing these fuels are highly energy intensive. This goes for second-generation cellulosic ethanol and biodiesel from algae as well. Research into synthetic biology pathways to biofuel production remains in its infancy.

Hydrogen offers a medium for storing energy in a way that can be used to power vehicles (among other things), and Toyota is about to release its first commercial hydrogen-powered car. But if we produce hydrogen with renewable energy, that means making H2 from water using solar or wind-based electricity; unfortunately, this is an expensive way to go about it (most commercially produced hydrogen is currently made from natural gas, because the gas-reforming process is inherently more efficient and therefore almost always cheaper than electrolysis, regardless of the electricity source).

These problems lead some energy analysts to propose a cheaper alternative to oil: why not transition the transport fleet to burn compressed natural gas, which government and industry tell us is abundant and climate-friendly? Unfortunately this is no solution at all over the long term. Globally, natural gas may be available in quantity for several more decades, but optimistic forecasts of "100 years" of abundant US domestic gas supplies are proving to be unfounded, and methane leakage from production and transmission infrastructure may end up making gas even worse for the climate than oil.

How Much Energy Will We Have?

The question is inescapable: will our renewable future offer less mobility? If so, this in itself would have enormous implications for the economy and for daily life. Another question arising from all of the above: will the *quantity* of energy available in our renewable-energy future match energy demand forecasts based on consumption trends in recent decades? There are too many variables to permit a remotely accurate estimate of *how much* less energy we might have to work with (we simply don't know how quickly renewable energy technology will evolve, or how much capital investment will materialize). However, it's good to keep in mind the fact that the energy transition of the 19th and 20th centuries was additive: we just kept piling new energy sources on top of existing ones (we started with firewood, then added coal, oil, hydropower, natural gas, and nuclear); further, it was driven by economic opportunity. In contrast, the energy transition of the 21st century will entail the *replacement* of our existing primary energy sources, and it may largely be driven either by government policy or by crisis (fuel scarcity, climate-induced weather disasters, or economic decline).

Even supply forecasts from renewable energy optimists who tell us that intermittency is affordably solvable typically assume we will have *less* available electrical energy, once the shift away from fossil fuels is complete, than the International Energy Agency estimates that we would otherwise want (for example, analysis by Lund and Mathieson projects energy consumption levels in 2030 in Denmark to be only 11 percent higher than 2004 demand, with no further increase between 2030 and 2050, whereas IEA forecasts assume continued demand growth through mid-century). However, if (as the Weissbach study suggests) intermittency is in fact a serious economic burden for solar and wind power over the long term, then we need to entertain the likelihood that energy supplies available at the end of the century may be smaller—maybe considerably smaller—than they are now.

At the same time, the *qualities* of our energy supply will differ from what we are used to. As explained earlier, solar and wind are intermittent, unlike fossil energy supplies. Further, while planet Earth is blessed with lots of wind and sunlight, these are diffuse energy sources that need collecting and concentrating if they're to operate heavy machinery. During the coming energy transition, we will be shifting from energy sources with a small geographic footprint (e.g., a natural gas well) toward ones with larger footprints (wind and solar farms collecting ambient sources of energy). True, we can cut the effective footprint of solar by using existing rooftops, and wind turbines can share space with food crops. Nevertheless, there will be unavoidable costs, inefficiencies, and environmental impacts resulting from the increasing geographical extent of energy collection activities.

The potency of fossil fuels derives from the fact that Nature did all the prior work of taking energy from sunlight, storing it in chemical bonds within plants, then gathering those ancient plants and transforming and concentrating their chemical energy, using enormous heat and pressure, over millions of years. Renewable energy technologies represent attempts to gather and concentrate ambient energy in present time, substituting built capital for Nature's free gifts.

Moreover, while electrical power is easily transported via the grid, this doesn't change the fact that sunlight, hydropower, biomass, and wind are more available in some places than others. Long-distance electricity transmission entails infrastructure costs and energy losses, while transporting biomass more than a hundred miles or so typically erases the crucial energy profitability of its use.

A Possible Outcome of Current Energy Trends

The price of renewable energy is falling while the cost of producing fossil fuels is rising. The crossover point, where fossil fuels cease to be cost competitive, could come soon—perhaps in the next decade.

What happens then? As batteries get cheaper, electric cars could become the industry standard; reduced gasoline demand would likely force the price of oil below its marginal production cost. If falling demand periodically outpaced declining supply (and vice versa), the result would be increasingly volatile petroleum prices, which would be bad for everyone. Meanwhile as more businesses and homes installed cost-competitive solar-and-battery systems, conventional utilities could go bankrupt.

The result: we would have green energy technology, but not the energy means to maintain and reproduce it over the long run (since every aspect of the renewable energy deployment process currently relies on fossil fuels —particularly oil— because of their unique energy density characteristics).

During the transition, what proportion of the world's people would be able to afford the up-front investment required for entry into the renewable energy club? It's likely that many (including poor people in rich countries) would not, especially given current trends toward increasing economic inequality; for these folks, conventional fossil-based grid power would likewise become unaffordable, or simply unavailable.

What if renewable energy optimists are right in saying that solar and wind are disruptive technologies against which fossil fuels cannot ultimately compete, but renewables critics are correct in arguing that solar and wind are inherently incapable of powering industrial societies as currently configured, absent a support infrastructure (mines, smelters, forges, ships, trucks, and so on) running on fossil fuels?

Googling Questions

The combined quantity and quality issues of our renewable energy future are sufficiently daunting that Google engineers who, in 2007, embarked on an ambitious, well-funded project to solve the world's climate and energy problems, effectively gave up. It seems that money, brainpower, and a willingness to think outside the box weren't enough. "We felt that with steady improvements to today's renewable energy technologies, our society could stave off catastrophic climate change," write Ross Koningstein and David Fork, key members of the RE<C project team. "We now know that to be a false hope."

The Google team defined "success" as identifying a renewable energy system that could compete economically with coal and could also be deployed fast enough to stave off the worst climate change impacts. The team concluded that renewable energy isn't up to that job. In their article, Koningstein and Fork put on a brave face, hoping that some currently unknown energy source will appear at the last minute to save the day. But putting one's faith in a currently non-existent energy source seems less realistic than working for dramatic improvements to solar and wind technologies. A completely new source would require decades for development, testing, and deployment. Realistically, our choice of replacements for fossil fuels is limited to energy sources that can be harnessed with current technology, even if they can't keep the industrial growth engine humming.

In inquiring whether renewable energy can solve the climate crisis at essentially no net economic cost, Koningstein and Fork may have been posing the wrong question. They were, in effect, asking whether renewables can support our current growth-based industrial economy while saving the environment. They might more profitably have inquired what kind of economy renewable energy *can* support. We humans got by on renewable sources of energy for millennia, achieving high levels of civilization and culture using wind, sun, water, wood, and animal power alone (though earlier civilizations often faced depletion dilemmas with regard to resources other than fossil fuels). The depletion/climate drawbacks of fossil fuels ensure that, as the century progresses, we will indeed return to a renewables-based economy of some sort, running on hydropower, solar, wind, and a suite of other, more marginal renewable sources including biomass, geothermal, wave, microhydro, and tidal power.

We always adapt our energy sources, as much as we can, to suit the ways we want to use energy. It is therefore understandable that most people would like somehow to make solar and wind act just like fossil fuels, which have shaped our current consumption patterns. But that leads us back to the problems of energy storage, capacity redundancy, grid redesign, transport electrification, and so on. Weissbach's study suggests that the costs of enabling solar and wind to act like fossil fuels are so great as to virtually cancel out these renewables' very real benefits. Reluctantly but increasingly, we may have to *adapt the ways we use energy* to suit the quantities and inherent qualities of the energy available to us.

Fossil fuels shaped our current infrastructure of mines, smelters, forges, factories, pipelines, grids, farms, highways, airports, pumps, shopping malls, suburbs, warehouses, furnaces, office buildings, houses, and more. We built the modern world with the assumption that we would always have more energy with similar characteristics to maintain, operate, and replace this staggering and still-growing array of machines, structures, and support systems. Where it is absolutely essential to maintain these systems in their current form, we will certainly make every effort to adapt our new energy sources to the job (using batteries, for example); where systems can themselves be adapted to using less energy or energy that is intermittently available, we will adapt those systems. But in many instances it may be unaffordable to adapt either the energy source or the usage system; in those cases, we will simply do without services we had become accustomed to.

This may be the renewable future that awaits us. To prepare for that likelihood, we need to build large numbers of solar panels and wind turbines while also beginning a process of industrial-economic triage.

Reconfiguring civilization to operate on less energy and on energy with different characteristics is a big job—one that, paradoxically, may itself require a substantial amount of energy. If the necessity of expending energy on a civilization rebuild coincides with a reduction in available energy, that would again mean that our renewable future will *not* be an extension of the expansive economic thrust of the 20th century. We may be headed into lean times.

Granted, there is a lot of uncertainty here. Some countries are better placed to harvest ambient natural energy sources than others. Some academic studies paint an over-optimistic picture of renewables, because they focus only on electricity and ignore or understate the costs of variability mitigation; other studies arrive at unfairly pessimistic assessments of renewables because they use obsolete price data. It's hard to portray our renewable future in a way that one analyst or another will not dispute, at least in terms of detail. Nevertheless, *most* energy experts would probably agree with the *general* outline of renewable energy's potential that I've traced here.

I consider myself a renewable energy advocate: after all, I work for an organization called Post Carbon Institute. I have no interest in discouraging the energy transition—quite the contrary. But I've concluded that many of us, like Koningstein and Fork, have been asking the wrong questions of renewables. We've been demanding that they continue to power a growth-based consumer economy that is inherently unsustainable for a variety of reasons (the most obvious one being that we live on a small planet with finite resources). The fact that renewables can't do that shouldn't actually be surprising.

What are the right questions? The first, already noted, is: What kind of society *can* up-to-date renewable energy sources power? The second, which is just as important: How do we go about becoming that sort of society?

As we'll see, once we begin to frame the picture this way, it turns out to be anything but bleak.

A Couple of Key Concepts

Our degree of success in this all-encompassing transition will partly depend on our ability to master a couple of simple energy concepts. The first is *energy returned on energy invested* (EROI or EROEI). It takes energy to get energy: for example, energy is needed to drill an oil well or build a solar panel. The historic economic bonanza resulting from society's use of fossil fuels partly ensued from the fact that, in the 20th century, only trivial amounts of energy were required for drilling or mining as compared to the gush of energy yielded. High EROEI ratios (in the range of 20:1 to 50:1 or more) for society's energy-obtaining efforts meant that relatively little capital and labor were needed in order to supply all the energy that society could use. As a result, many people could be freed up from basic energy-producing activities (like farming), their labor being substituted by fuel-fed machines. Channeled into manufacturing and managerial jobs, these people found ways to use abundant, cheap energy to produce more goods and services. The middle class mushroomed, as did cities and suburbs. In the process, we discovered an unintended consequence of having an abundance of cheap "energy slaves" in the forms of tons of coal, barrels of oil, and cubic feet of natural gas: as manufacturing and other sectors of the economy became mechanized, many pre-industrial professions disappeared.

The EROEI ratios for fossil fuels are declining because the best-quality resources are being used up; meanwhile, the energy return figures of most renewable energy sources are relatively low compared to fossil fuels in their heyday (and this is especially true when buffering technologies—such as storage equipment, redundant capacity, and grid expansions—are accounted for).

The practical result of *declining overall societal EROEI will be the need to devote proportionally more capital and labor to energy production processes.* This is likely to translate, for example, to the requirement for more farm labor, and to fewer opportunities in professions not centered on directly productive activities: we'll need more people making or growing things, and fewer people marketing, advertising, financing, regulating, and litigating them. For folks who think we have way too much marketing, advertising, financialization, regulation, and litigation in our current society, this may not seem like such a bad thing; prospects are likewise favorable for those who desire more control over their time, labor, and sources of sustenance (food and energy).

A second essential energy concept has to do with the difference between embodied and operational energy. When we contemplate the energy required by an automobile, for example, we are likely to think only of the gasoline in its tank. However, a substantial amount of energy was expended in the car's construction, in the mining of ores from which its metal components were made, in the making of the mining equipment, and so on. Further, enormous amounts of energy were spent in building the infrastructure that enables us to use the car—the systems of roads and highways, the networks of service stations, refineries, pipelines, and oil wells. The car's gasoline supplies operational energy, but much more energy is embodied in the car itself and its support systems. This latter energy expenditure is easily overlooked.

The energy glut of the 20th century enabled us to embody energy in a mind-numbing array of buildings, infrastructure, machines, gadgets, and packaging. Middle-class families got used to buying and discarding enormous quantities of manufactured goods representing generous portions of previously expended energy. If we have less energy available to us in our renewable future, this will impact more than the operation of our machines and the lighting and heating of our buildings. It will also translate to a shrinking flow of manufactured goods that embody past energy expenditure, and a reduced ability to construct high energy-input structures. We might find we need to purchase fewer items of clothing and furniture, and fewer electronic devices, and inhabit smaller spaces. We might also use old goods longer, and re-use and re-purpose whatever can be repaired. We might need to get used to buying more basic foods again, rather than highly processed and excessively packaged food products. Exactly how far these trends might proceed is impossible to say: we are almost surely headed toward a simpler society, but no one knows ultimately how simple. Nevertheless, it's fair to assume that this overall shift would constitute the end of consumerism (i.e., our current economic model that depends on ever-increasing consumption of consumer goods and services). Here again, there are more than a few people who believe that advanced industrial nations consume excessively, and that some simplification of rich- and middle-class lifestyles would be a good thing.

Transitioning Nine Sectors

Food: Fossil fuels are currently used at every stage of growing, transporting, processing, packaging, preparing, and storing food. As those inputs are removed from food systems, it will be necessary to bring growers and consumers closer together, and to replace petrochemical-based fertilizers, herbicides, and pesticides with agro-ecological farming methods that rely on crop rotation, intercropping, companion planting, mulching, composting, beneficial insects, and promotion of microbial activity in soils. As mentioned earlier, we will need many more farmers, especially ones with extensive practical, local ecological knowledge.

Water: Enormous amounts of energy are used in extracting, moving, and treating water; conversely, water is used in most energy production processes. We face converging water crises arising from aging infrastructure and climate change-related droughts and floods. All this suggests we must become far more water thrifty, find ways to reduce the energy used in water management, use intermittent energy sources for pumping water, and use water reservoirs for storing energy.

Resource extraction (mining, forestry, fishing): Currently, extractive industries rely almost entirely on petroleum-based fuels. Since, as we have seen, there are no good and comprehensive substitutes for these fuels, we will have to reduce resource extraction rates, reuse and recycle materials wherever possible, and employ more muscle power where possible in those extractive processes that must continue (such as forestry).

Building construction: Cement, iron, and road-building materials embody substantial amounts of energy, while large construction equipment (cranes, booms, bulldozers) requires concentrated energy for its operation. We must shift to using natural, locally available building materials, and more labor-intensive construction methods, while dramatically reducing the rate of new construction. The amount of enclosed space per person (home, work, shopping) will shrink.

Building operations: We've gotten used to actively heating, cooling, ventilating, and lighting our buildings with cheap, on-demand energy. We will need to maximize our passive capture of ambient, variable, solar energy using south-facing glazing, superinsulation, and thermal mass. Whatever active energy use is still required will employ efficient heat pumps and low-energy LED lighting, powered mostly by solar cells and wind turbines with minimal storage and redundancy (so as to maximize EROEI).

Manufacturing: Our current system is globalized (relying on oil-based transport systems); consumes natural gas, electricity, and oil in manufacturing processes; and uses materials that embody large amounts of energy and that are often made from fossil fuels (i.e., plastics). Lots of energy is used also in dealing with substantial flows of waste in the forms of packaging and discarded products. The economy has been fine-tuned to maximize consumption. We must shift to shortened supply chains, more localized manufacture of goods (shipping information, not products), materials with low embodied energy, and minimal packaging, while increasing our products' reuse and repair potential. This will be, in effect, an economy fine-tuned to minimize consumption.

Health care: The high dollar cost of modern health care is a rough indication of its energy intensity. As the energy transition gains momentum, it will be necessary to identify low-energy sanitation and care options, and prioritize prevention and local disaster response preparedness. Eventually, high-energy diagnostics and extreme end-of-life interventions may simply become unaffordable. Treatment of chronic conditions may rely increasingly on herbs and other traditional therapies (in instances where their efficacy can be verified) as the pharmaceutical industry gradually loses its capability to mobilize billions of dollars to develop new, targeted drugs.

Transportation: The energy transition will require us to prioritize transport modes according to operational and embodied energy efficiency: whereas automobile and truck traffic have been richly subsidized through road building in the last seven decades, governments should instead devote funds toward electrified rail networks for both freight and passenger travel. We must also design economic and urban systems so as to reduce the need for motorized transportation—for example, by planning communities so that most essential services are within walking distance.

Finance: It would appear that comparatively little energy is needed to run financial systems, as a few taps on a computer keyboard can create millions of dollars instantly and move them around the globe. Nevertheless, the energy transition has enormous implications for finance: heightened debt levels imply an increased ability to consume now with the requirement to pay later. In effect, a high-finance society stimulates consumption, whereas we need to reduce consumption. Transition strategies should therefore include goals such as the cancelation of much existing debt and reduction of the size and role of the financial system. Increasingly, we must direct investment capital toward projects that will tangibly benefit communities, rather than leaving capital investment primarily in the hands of profit-seeking individuals and corporations.

You may have noticed that suggestions in each of these categories are far from new. Organized efforts to reduce both operational and embodied energy consumption throughout society started in the 1970s, at the time of the first oil price shocks. Today there are many NGOs and university programs devoted to research on energy efficiency, and to life cycle analysis (which seeks to identify and quantify energy consumption and environmental impacts of products and industrial processes, from "cradle to grave"). Industrial ecology, biomimicry, "cradle-to-cradle" manufacturing, local food, voluntary simplicity, permaculture, and green building are just a few of the strategies have emerged in the last few decades to guide us toward a more energy-thrifty future. Most major cities now have bicycle advocacy groups, farmers markets, and energy efficiency programs. These all represent steps in the right direction.

Yet what is being done so far barely scratches the surface of what's needed. There could be only one meaningful indication of success in all these efforts, and that would be a decline in society's overall energy use. So far, we have seen energy declines primarily in times of severe economic recession—hardly ever purely as a result efficiency programs. What we need is not just to trim energy use here and there so as to save money, but to reconfigure entire systems to dramatically slash consumption while making much of the remaining energy consumption amenable to intermittent inputs.

Another insight that comes from scanning energy reduction strategies in various societal sectors is that efforts already underway along these lines often have side benefits. There are tangible psychological, social, and cultural payoffs associated with local food and voluntary simplicity programs, and health improvements can follow from natural, energy-efficient dwellings, walking, bicycling, and gardening. A successful energy transition will require that we find ways to maximize and celebrate these benefits, while honestly acknowledging the full human and environmental costs of our decades-long, fossil-fueled joyride.

In the march toward our energy future, the PR war between the fossil fuel industry and renewables advocates gets much of the attention. But it will be our effectiveness in the hard work of dramatically reducing and reconfiguring energy consumption—sector by sector, farm by farm, building by building, household by household, community by community—that will largely determine our overall success in what is likely to be history's most difficult and crucially important economic shift.

Neither Utopia Nor Extinction

This is all politically charged. Some renewable energy advocates (particularly in the US) soft-pedal the "use less" message because we still inhabit an economy in which jobs and profits depend on stoking consumption, not cutting it. "Less" also implies "fewer": if the amount of energy available contracts but human population continues growing, that will translate to an even sharper *per capita* hit. This suggests we need to start reducing population, and doing so quickly—but economists hate population decline because it compromises GDP and results in smaller generational cohorts of young workers supporting larger cohorts of retirees. Here is yet another message that just doesn't sell. A contraction of energy, population, and the economy has only two things going for it: necessity and inevitability.

From a political standpoint, some solar and wind advocates apparently believe it makes good strategic sense to claim that a renewable future will deliver comfort, convenience, jobs, and growth—an extension of the oil-fueled 20th century, but now energized by wind and solar electrons. Regardless of whether it's true, it is a message that appeals to a broad swath of the public. Yet most serious renewable energy scientists and analysts acknowledge that the energy transition will require changes throughout society. This latter attitude is especially prevalent in Europe, which now has practical experience integrating larger percentages of solar and wind power into electricity markets. Here in the US, though, it is common to find passionate but poorly informed climate activists who loudly proclaim that the transition can be easily and fully accomplished at no net cost. Again, this may be an effective message for rallying troops, but it ends up denying oxygen to energy conservation efforts, which are just as important.

I have good friends in the renewable energy industry who say that emphasizing the intermittency challenges of solar and wind amounts to giving more ammunition to the fossil fuel lobby. Barry Goldwater famously proclaimed that "Extremism in the defense of liberty is no vice;" in a similar spirit, some solar and wind boosters might say that a little exaggeration of renewable energy's potential, uttered in defense of the Earth, is no sin. After all, fossil fuel interests are not bound by the need for strict veracity: they continually make absurd claims that the world has centuries' worth of coal and gas, and decades of oil. It's not a fair or equal fight: the size and resources of the fossil fuel industry vastly outweigh those of the renewables camp. And there could hardly be more at stake: this is war for the survival of our current civilization-supporting climate regime. Nevertheless, we will ultimately have to deal with the reality of what solar and wind can actually provide, and we will do so far more successfully if we plan and prepare ahead of time.

There are a lot of smart, dedicated people working hard to solve the problems with renewables—that is, to make it cheaper and easier for these energy sources to mimic the 24/7 reliability of fossil fuels through improvements in energy storage and related technologies. None of what I have said in this essay is meant to discourage them from that important work. The more progress they make, the better for all of us. But they'll have more chance of success in the long run if society starts investing significant effort into adapting its energy usage to lower consumption levels, more variable sources, and more localized, distributed inputs.

The problem is, the gap between our current way of life and one that can be sustained with future energy supplies is likely to be significant. If energy declines, so will economic activity, and that will create severe political and geopolitical strains; arguably some of those are already becoming apparent. We may be headed into a crucial bottleneck; if so, our decisions now will have enormous repercussions. We therefore need an honest view of the constraints and opportunities ahead.

At this point I must address a few words to "collapsitarians" or "doomers," who say that only utter ruin, perhaps extinction, awaits us, and that renewables won't work at all. They may be correct in thinking that the trajectory of society this century will be comparable to the collapse of historic civilizations. However, even if that is the case, there is still a wide range of possible futures. The prospects for humanity, and the fates of many other species, hang on our actions.

What's needed now is neither fatalism nor utopianism, but a suite of practical pathways for families and communities that lead to a real and sustainable renewable future—parachutes that will get us from a 17,000-watt society to a 2,000-watt society. We need public messages that emphasize the personal and community benefits of energy conservation, and visions of an attractive future where human needs are met with a fraction of the operational and embodied energy that industrial nations currently use. We need detailed transition plans for each major sector of the economy. We need inspiring examples, engaging stories, and opportunities for learning in depth. The transition to our real renewable future deserves a prominent, persistent place at the center of public conversation.

The Transition Network, The Arthur Morgan Institute for Community Solutions, The Simplicity Institute, and many other organizations have already begun pioneering this work, and deserve support and attention. However, more framing and analysis of the issues, along the lines of this essay but in much greater depth, could also help. My organization, Post Carbon Institute, is embarking on a collaborative project to provide this. If you don't hear much from me for a while, it's because I'm working on it. Stay tuned.

Notes

*For the sake of simplicity, I have omitted discussion of nuclear power from this essay. There are those who say that nuclear power will, or should, play a prominent role in our energy future. I disagree with this view. Globally, nuclear power—unlike solar and wind—is contracting, not growing (China provides one of only a few exceptions to this observation). Nations are turning away from nuclear power due to the high levels of required investment—which, in virtually every case, must be underwritten by government. They are doing so also because of the high perceived risk of accidents—especially since the commencement of the ongoing catastrophe at the Fukushima nuclear facility in Japan. Nuclear boosters advocate new fuels (thorium) or technologies (fast breeder reactors) to address these concerns. But many years of trials will be needed before these alternatives are ready to be deployed at scale; and it is unclear, even then, whether they will live up to claims and expectations.

Organizations to Contact

The editors have compiled the following list of organizations concerned with the issues debated in this book. The descriptions are derived from materials provided by the organizations. All have publications or information available for interested readers. The list was compiled on the date of publication of the present volume; the information provided here may change. Be aware that many organizations take several weeks or longer to respond to inquiries, so allow as much time as possible.

The Breakthrough Institute
436 14th Street, Suite 820
Oakland, CA 94612
phone: (510) 550-8800
email: info@thebreakthrough.org
website: www.thebreakthrough.org

The Breakthrough Institute has a mission to change the way people think about the environment. Through pioneering research they hope to spread understanding about energy and to encourage a sustainable future for the planet.

Canadian Association of Petroleum Producers
2100, 350 7 Avenue SW
Calgary, AL T2P 3N9
Canada
phone: (403) 267-1100
email: communication@capp.ca
website: www.capp.ca

The Canadian Association of Petroleum Producers (CAPP) is a group that advocates for the natural gas and oil industry in Canada. Their goal is to achieve competitive economic practice with safe environmental and social performance.

Center for American Progress
1333 H Street NW, 10th Floor
Washington, DC 20005
phone: (202) 682-1611
website: www.americanprogress.org

The Center for American Progress is a policy institute that encourages national debate. Through leadership and action this agency promotes an agenda working towards global peace, prosperity and protection of the environment for future generations.

The Heritage Foundation
214 Massachusetts Avenue NE
Washington, DC 20002-4999
phone: (202) 546-4400
email: info@heritage.org
website: www.heritage.org

The Heritage Foundation is an organization that promotes research and education. They aim to encourage conservative public policies based on traditional values, freedom, strong system of defense, and free enterprise.

International Energy Agency
31-35 rue de la Fédération
75739 Paris Cedex 15 France
email: info@iea.org
website: www.iea.org

The International Energy Agency works to provide reliable, clean, and affordable energy for all its members. They promote education through workshops, webinars, videos, and more, working towards an understanding of global energy.

Manhattan Institute
52 Vanderbilt Avenue
New York, NY 10017
phone: (212) 599-7000
email: info@manhattaninstitute.org
website: www.manhattan-institute.org

The Manhattan Institute (MI) is a think tank focusing on various issues including energy and the environment. Their aim is to help shape and improve American political and economic culture. A staff of experts spreads information through publications, conferences, radio, and T.V. The Institute will also sends teams to cities and states to help officials when requested.

National Energy Board
505 De Maisonneuve Boulevard West, Suite 230
Montreal, QC H3A 3C2
Canada
phone: (877) 288-8803
email: infomontreal@neb-one.gc.ca
website: www.neb-one.gc.ca/index-eng.html

The National Energy Board is a Canadian organization engaged in regulation of energy development, trade, and pipelines throughout Canada. By taking into account economic, environmental, and social issues, they pursue a sustainable energy future for all Canadians.

Natural Gas Supply Association
1620 Eye Street NW, Suite 700
Washington, DC 20006
phone: (202) 326-9300
website: www.naturalgas.org

The Natural Gas Supply Association maintains the comprehensive, unbiased informational website listed above to educate students, teachers, government officials, the general public and the media about the energy source of natural gas. This agency works to ensure safe, reliable energy in the form of natural gas to consumers. They seek to maintain a competitive market for customers, and appropriate regulations in the industry.

Natural Resources Defense Council (NRDC)
40 West 20th Street, 11th floor
New York, NY 10011
Phone: (212) 727-2700
email: nrdcinfo@nrdc.org
website: www.nrdc.org

The Natural Resources Defense Council along with its scientists, lawyers, and advocates, is an organization dedicated to working with businesses, officials, and communities on many important issues including climate, clean air, energy, transportation, science, and the environment.

Post Carbon Institute
613 4th Street, Suite #208,
Santa Rosa, CA 95404
phone: (707) 823-8700
email: info@postcarbon.org
website: www.postcarbon.org/

The Post Carbon Institute promotes the use of renewable energy sources, along with a message of understanding about the need to reduce energy consumption. The Institute believes that energy, ecology, economy, and equity are intertwined, and wants to lead, and instruct communities and individuals on how to best implement these issues and ideas.

US Department of Energy
1000 Independence Avenue SW
Washington, DC 20585
phone: (202) 586-5000
email: The.Secretary@hq.doe.gov
website: energy.gov

The mission of the Energy Department is to provide for America's well being through a safe and secure energy supply, and remedy challenges through science and technology. As a leader in science they support research in the National Laboratories aimed at new clean energy technologies.

US Energy Information Administration (EIA)
1000 Independence Avenue SW
Washington, DC 20585
phone: (202) 586-8800
website: www.eia.gov

The Energy Information Administration and its staff collect, analyze, and distribute information about energy. They promote public understanding of energy and how it relates to the economy and the environment. It is an independent governmental agency.

Bibliography

Books

Samuel Avery. *The Pipeline and the Paradigm: Keystone XL, Tar Sands, and the Battle to Diffuse the Carbon Bomb.* Washington, D.C.: Ruka Press, 2013.

Keith Barnhan. *The Burning Answer: The Solar Revolution: A Quest for Sustainable Power.* New York, NY: Pegasus Books, 2015.

Toban Black, Tony Weis, Stephen D'Arcy, and Joshua Kahn Russell, editors. *A Line in the Tar Sands: Struggles for Environmental Justice.* Oakland, CA: PM Press, 2014.

Ronald H. Bowman Jr. *The Green Guide to Power: Thinking Outside the Grid.* Charleston, SC: Booksurge.com, 2008.

Lester Brown. *The Great Transition: Shifting from Fossil Fuels to Solar and Wind Energy.* New York, NY: W. W. Norton & Company, 2015.

Robert W. Collin. *The Environmental Protection Agency: Cleaning Up America's Act.* Westport, CT: Greenwood Press, 2006.

David Craddock. *Renewable Energy Made Easy: Free Energy from Solar, Wind, Hydropower, and other Alternative Energy Sources.* Ocala, FL: Atlantic Publishing Group, 2008.

Tim Flannery. *Atmosphere of Hope: Searching for Solutions to the Climate Crisis.* New York, NY: Grove Press, 2016.

Dieter Helm. *Burn Out: The Endgame for Fossil Fuels.* New Haven, CT: Yale University Press, 2017.

Paul Kruger. *Alternative Energy Resources: The Quest for Sustainable Energy.* Hoboken, NJ: John Wiley, 2006.

Richard Martin. *Coal Wars: The Future of Energy and the Fate of the Planet.* New York, NY: Palgrave Macmillin, 2015.

Stephen Moore. *Fueling Freedom: Exposing the Mad War on Energy.* Washington, DC: Regnery Publishing, 2016.

Andrea C. Nakaya. *America in the Twenty-First Century.* Farmington Hills, MI: Greenhaven Press, 2006.

Joseph Powers. *The Energy Problem.* Hackensack, NJ: World Scientific Publishing, 2011.

Tom Rand. *Kick the Fossil Fuel Habit: 10 Clean Technologies to Save Our World.* Toronto, Canada: Eco Ten Publishing, 2010.

Tamara Thompson, book editor. *Oil Spills.* Detroit, MI: Greenhaven Press, 2014.

Marek Walisiewicz. *Alternative Energy.* New York, NY: DK Publishing, 2002.

Periodicals and Internet Sources

Alex Altman, "The Thin Green Line," *Time,* February 15, 2016.

Adnan Z. Amin, "How Renewable Energy Can Be Cost-Competitive," *UN Chronicle,* December 2015. https://unchronicle.un.org/article/how-renewable-energy-can-be-cost-competitive.

Brendan F. D. Barrett, "Energy Descent from Peak Oil: Collapse or Evolution?" *Our World,* November 13, 2009. https://ourworld.unu.edu/en/creative-energy-descent.

Natasha Bernal, "Canada: Green Gold," *The Lawyer,* February 6, 2017. https://www.thelawyer.com/issues/6-february-2017/canada-green-gold/.

Russell A. Carter, "Cashing in on Renewable Energy," *Engineering & Mining Journal,* April 27, 2017. http://www.e-mj.com/features/6820-cashing-in-on-renewable-energy.html#.WXJnSumQzIU.

Petr Cizek, "Scouring Scum and Tar from the Bottom of the Pit," *Canadian Dimension,* July 9, 2006. https://canadiandimension.com/articles/view/scouring-scum-and-tar-from-the-bottom-of-the-pit-peter-cizek.

E & C Press Release, "Real Solutions to Protect and Create Jobs," *The Energy and Commerce Committee,* January 5, 2012. https://energycommerce.house.gov/news-center/press-releases/real-solutions-protect-and-create-jobs.

Ron Johnson, "Nations Rising," *Earth Island Journal,* Winter 2017. http://www.earthisland.org/journal/index.php/eij/article/nations_rising/.

Tim Miser, "Puzzle Pieces: The Place of Renewables in an Evolving Energy Landscape," January 24, 2017. http://www.power-eng.com/articles/print/volume-121/issue-1/features/puzzle-pieces-the-place-of-renewables-in-an-evolving-energy-landscape.html.

Richard Nemec, "2017 Shaping Up as a Time to Build Pipelines," *Pipeline & Gas Journal,* May 2017. https://pgjonline. com/2017/05/02/2017-shaping-up-as-a-time-to-build-pipelines/.

Andrew Nikiforuk, "Sticky Business," *New Internationalist,* March 2014.

Sergey Paltsev, "The Complicated Geopolitics of Renewable Energy," *Bulletin of the Atomic Scientists,* November 1, 2016. http:// thebulletin.org/2016/november/complicated-geopolitics-renewable-energy10112.

Sara Phillips, "Beyond the Grid," *Australian Geographic,* July-August, 2016. http://www.australiangeographic.com.au/magazine/ archive/volume_133/ag133-085.

Wen Stephenson, "The Grassroots Battle Against Big Oil," *The Nation,* October 9, 2013. https://www.thenation.com/article/grassroots-battle-against-big-oil/.

Letha Tawney, "Electric Perspectives: Innovative Partnerships Deliver Renewable Energy," *Corporate Renewable Energy Buyers' Principles,* January 5, 2016. http://buyersprinciples. org/2016/01/05/electric-perspectives-innovative-partnerships-deliver-renewable-energy/.

Suez Taylor and Sadie Luetmer, "Pushing Back on Pipelines," *Progressive,* October 28, 2016. http://progressive.org/magazine/ pushing-back-pipelines/.

Michael P. Voelker, "The Future's So Bright," *Property Casulty 360,* July 25, 2016. http://www.propertycasualty360. com/2016/07/25/future-is-bright-for-renewable-energy-market?slreturn=1500671093.

Ken Ward, "No Regrets," *Earth Island Journal,* Summer 2017. http:// www.earthisland.org/journal/index.php/eij/article/no_regrets/.

Index

3